UNDER
THE DRAGON

CALIFORNIA'S NEW CULTURE

UNDER THE DRAGON

CALIFORNIA'S NEW CULTURE

LONNY SHAVELSON AND FRED SETTERBERG
PHOTOGRAPHY BY LONNY SHAVELSON

OAKLAND MUSEUM OF CALIFORNIA, OAKLAND, CALIFORNIA
HEYDAY BOOKS, BERKELEY, CALIFORNIA

© 2007 by Lonny Shavelson and Fred Setterberg
Foreword © 2007 by Andrew Lam

Library of Congress Cataloging-in-Publication Data

Shavelson, Lonny.
  Under the dragon : California's new culture /
Lonny Shavelson and
Fred Setterberg ; photography by Lonny Shavelson.
    p. cm.
  ISBN 1-59714-045-7 (pbk. : alk. paper)
1. Pluralism (Social sciences)--California--San
Francisco Bay Area. 2. Minorities--California--
San Francisco Bay Area. 3. Intercultural com-
munication--California--San Francisco Bay Area.
4. Community life--California--San Francisco Bay
Area. 5. Neighborhood-- California--San Francisco
Bay Area. 6. San Francisco Bay Area (Calif.)--
Social life and customs. 7. San Francisco Bay Area
(Calif.)--Social conditions. 8. San Francisco Bay
Area (Calif.)-- Ethnic relations. 9. Minorities--
California--San Francisco Bay Area-- Pictorial
works. 10. San Francisco Bay Area (Calif.)--Social
life and customs--Pictorial works. I. Setterberg,
Fred. II. Title.
  F868.S156S47 2007
  305.8009794'6--dc22
                                    2006017717

Cover Art: *Kenneth Buncum lion dancing at the
St. Patrick's Day parade, San Francisco*

Cover Design: Toki Design
Interior Design/Typesetting: Toki Design

Printed in Singapore by Imago

Co-published by Heyday Books and the Oakland
Museum of California. Orders, inquiries, and
correspondence should be addressed to:
    Heyday Books
    P. O. Box 9145, Berkeley, CA 94709
    (510) 549-3564, Fax (510) 549-1889
    www.heydaybooks.com

10 9 8 7 6 5 4 3 2 1

To Patrick, Angela, Sofia Xitlali, and Carlos Thanh—new Californians all

CONTENTS

ACKNOWLEDGMENTS

WE THANK OUR FRIENDS AND COLLEAGUES WHO SUPPORTED THIS PROJECT IN SO
many ways: June Anderson, for sharing her remarkable Traditional Arts Calendar; Kim Bancroft, for
editing and caring; Paul and Monica Bancroft, for listening to the stories over and over again; Deborah
Bickel; William Dial; David Early; Joan Emery and Marina Crouse, gracias por escuchar las historias;
Renee Emunah; Marla Lev; William Levin; Ken Light; Melanie Light; all the students from Fotovi-
sion; Meredith Maran; Scott McKiernan and the staff at Zuma Press; Laurie McWhorter; Susan Parker;
Elizabeth Partridge, who introduced this project to Heyday; Philip Arca, Fred Goff, Kim Hsieh, Ernest
Landauer, Ralph Lewin, Marjorie Schwarzer, and Chuck Wollenberg, for their wise counsel and conversation; Wendy Ellen Ledger, for her never-failing attention to detail; Marshall Krantz for his expert
direction; Mitchell Schwarzer, for his careful reading and commentary; Naomi Porat, for her work with
the Pacific Coast Immigration Museum; The S&M Writing Group: Martin Bennett, Maureen Murdock,
Melita Schaum, Jan Stürmann; Stacy Rosenstock; and the dedicated photographers at Impact Digitals;
and, in so much as always, Ann Van Steenberg.

Many thanks to the folks in public radio, where this project (and others) will continue on: Alisa
Barba at NPR; Margo Melnicove—mentor extraordinaire at NPR, then at BBC/PRI's The World; Ingrid
Becker and Scott Shafer at The California Report; Faith Lapidus at Voice of America; Michelle Levander
at the Annenberg School for Communication; and Bari Scott at SoundVision.

Thanks also to Malcolm Margolin, Jeannine Gendar, and the staff at Heyday, who guided us
in transforming this project into a book; Mark Medeiros and Christiaan Klieger at the Oakland
Museum of California, who figured out how to make the book come alive on their museum walls;
James LeBrecht, for bringing sound to the images and stories; and Michiko Toki, for her remarkable
talents in book design.

Most of all, sincere gratitude to the many, many people throughout the greater San Francisco Bay
Area who generously spoke to us about their lives over the past three years.

I

MY FIRST CALIFORNIA MOMENT: I AM TWELVE YEARS OLD. I DO NOT yet speak English, only Vietnamese and French. Fresh from the Pendleton refugee camp, I am quickly enrolled in an ESL class in summer school in Colma, south of San Francisco. On our second day we all learn to parrot this phrase: *I am from…* Thus, shyly, in various accents, the world introduces itself…

…the Philippines.

…Mexico.

…Nicaragua.

…Greece.

…Taiwan.

…*Vietnam.*

For the summer I am wedged between Mexico and Taiwan. Taiwan is timid and bookish, but boisterous Mexico, whose name is Juan, and I immediately bond. Communicating with our hands, facial gestures, and a few shared words, we manage to joke and banter. "I am from Mexico," Juan keeps whispering in various cadences, as if trying out a new song, until I fall into a fit of giggles. Mrs. H., our teacher, who is beautiful and blond, and married to a black man from Africa (she shows us pictures of her wedding the first day), makes us sit outside of the classroom for disrupting the class.

And here's the moment: a redhead stops by as Juan continues his antics outside. "I'm from here," she says, and then she shakes our hands as if we had just landed on the tarmac. "Welcome to America," she says. She then gives us each a stick of cinnamon gum. Juan and I look at each other, and shrug. I pop the gum in my mouth and chew. Spicy. Sweet.

Three decades later I can finally say what I intuited at that piquant instant: to live in the Bay Area, where I am now from, is to live at the crossroads of a global society. It's many a tourist's mistake to define the place materially, and it is true that the things it is known for—arching bridges and grand ports and famed high-tech companies—evoke, in many ways, what often transpires here: the ability to span distances and transgress borders.

A magnificent terrain, certainly, and full of golden promises, but so much more: a place where human restlessness and fabulous alchemical commingling are becoming increasingly the norm. The entire world comes to the Bay Area, and the Bay Area, in return, assimilates the world. The Central Pacific Railroad ended here, but more than a century and half later, the majority of the construction of that far-reaching new undertaking, the information highway—Yahoo, Google, IBM, eBay, Sun Microsoft, Cisco Systems, Craigslist, Apple, Pixar, Netscape, Intel, Oracle, and a myriad of others—while centered here, is everywhere, virtually.

Gertrude Stein once observed about Oakland, where she spent her childhood, that "there's no there there." But having grown up here and traveled the world, I'd like to add this corollary: nowhere is as both here and there as the Bay Area.

Go to the San Francisco Airport on any given day and you'll see what I mean. A world in motion, in flux: the number of people who pass through those gates at SFO each year exceeds the entire population of the Golden State. At last count, Census 2000, there were 112 languages spoken in the Bay Area, and 80 in the thirty-square-mile city of Richmond, population one hundred thousand. On warm summer afternoons, Nob Hill, where I live, turns into the modern Tower of Babel. The languages of the world—Chinese, French, Spanish, German, Russian, Thai, Japanese, Hindi, Vietnamese, and many more I do not recognize—waft in through my open windows, accompanied by the cable cars' merry cling-clanging bells.

These days Shanghai, Bombay, Cairo, Paris, Buenos Aires, and the likes are much closer to the Bay Area than we ever thought possible. There's a transnational revolution taking place, one right beneath our noses. The teenage girl in Marin County is flirting in the chat room with the teenage boy in Islamabad. The Chinese businessman in Silicon Valley is talking to his grandmother in Guangdong on his cell, while answering e-mails from his business partners in London and Rio de Janeiro. And when a woman at a cocktail party told me casually that she was bicoastal, she did not mean the tired New York–San Francisco trajectory. She summers in San Francisco but winters in Shanghai.

Or try on this scene, another California moment: in their high-ceilinged SoMa flat, two friends of mine are conversing with the world. An Austrian H1B Silicon Valley computer wiz chats with his parents in Vienna on his webcam; his Singaporean boyfriend, who is holding his hand, is gossiping in mixed Mandarin and English on his cell phone with his sister in Melbourne. On TV, which neither one is watching at the moment, characters from their favorite Japanese anime are fighting a bloody battle in some futuristic metropolis.

California's diversity is, of course, nothing new. Multiracial, multicultural, and multilingual—even if differences were not historically celebrated, all these delineations were part of the Golden State from the get-go. Latin and Anglo America came to an epic collision, and California was the result.

Long before Webster acknowledged the word, globalization had already swept over the Bay Area. Gold made the state famous around the world, and the world rushed in and greeted itself, perhaps for the first time. Since then layers upon layers of complexity—tastes, architecture, religions, animals, plants, stories, music, languages—have been piled onto the place, making it in many ways postmodern even before the rest of the world struggled to enter the modern era.

Before I came to San Francisco I too knew it, as most East Asians knew it, as Old Gold Mountain, with the Golden Gate as entrance to a wondrous America. Living on that mountain now, I too have seen my share of the gold rush made new by microchips and startup companies. "Try to imagine," a Vietnamese American entrepreneur friend of mine, once a refugee, tells me, "a new wave of Indians and Chinese and Vietnamese software programmers building the information highway, and you have the repeat of when poor Chinese laborers were building the railroad." Except for this: he retired at thirty-eight, having sold his startup company, and now manages his portfolio and collects art.

Diversity may not be new, but it has certainly been intensified by the degree of interactions, and by the rate of change we are all experiencing due to the forces of globalization. And new too is the way our society has gone from being overtly xenophobic—many Chinese railroad workers were murdered when they finished building the railroad—to celebratory about our differences. While racism will always lurk in many a resenting heart, and fear of the other will always be part of the human condition, cultures that were once considered proprietary have spilled irrevocably into the mainstream, mixing with one another, transforming the landscape.

Think about it: three decades ago, who would have thought that sushi—raw fish—would become an indelible part of California cuisine? Or that Vietnamese fish sauce would be found down Aisle 3 of Safeway? Or that salsa would be replacing ketchup as the most-consumed sauce?

The *San Francisco Chronicle* the other day had this article on its front page: "America's mean cuisine: more like it hot—from junk food to ethnic dishes, spicy flavors are the rage." We slowly give up blandness to savor the pungent lemongrass in our soup, feel that tangy burn of red curry on the tongue. Tomorrow's classics are today's bold experiments: tofu burrito, hummus guacamole, spring rolls with salsa dipping sauce, lamb in tamarind sauce, lychee martini, wasabi bloody mary.

In my lifetime here I have watched the pressure to move toward some generic, standardized melting-potted center deflate—transpose, in fact—to something quite its opposite, as the demography shifts toward a society in which there's no discernible majority, no clear single center. I notice, of course, the region's undeniable Asian flare. So it's not surprising that Kevin, otherwise of Germanic ancestry, is so impressed by the Orient. Or rather, the Orient has for a while now impressed itself upon him. In a Thai restaurant the other day, he scowled at the French tourist's struggle with her chopsticks over a bowl of shrimp noodle at the next table—a single chopstick in each well-manicured hand as if she were about to knit. "I have to say, that f**king offends me! It's just so un–San Franciscan."

Which made me laugh. Something about Kevin's unabashed insistence that chopstick etiquette should be essential to Bay Area living makes it at once honest and somehow radical. Which is to also say, if I once felt ashamed of my parents' singsong accents or my mother's strong-scented cooking, or my own Vietnamese memories, I see them now as a norm, as regional colors, if not assets. Ethnic is chic in a metropolis that grows increasingly horizontal, where ethnic festivals and parades are celebrated publicly with everyone else participating and cheering, and in my mind's eye, they crisscross and stretch into one another, amalgamating toward a hopeful future shimmering at the horizon.

II

OR PUT IT THIS WAY: THE BAY AREA IS A PLACE WHERE, AS *UNDER THE DRAGON* authors Lonny Shavelson and Fred Setterberg note, "People come together, often inadvertently, to confound narrow expectations about race and culture."

If I have the pleasure and fortune to write the foreword for this illuminating book, it's because it polymorphously tells of my own American (or should I say Bay Arean?) biography. Part historical, part anthropological, *Under the Dragon* is over all a kind of tour guide to what the authors call "an unfamiliar country." The photos and accompanying stories capture much of the dynamic of the new millennium in the Bay Area, where the experiment of pluralism is at full tilt.

From the book, one sees that something of the Old World has reconstituted itself in the new, and some traditions are seemingly preserved. Yet at closer look one also glimpses the enormous options and paradoxes at play. While Old World vehemence is still present in some New World settings—for instance, Vietnamese vets still wear South Vietnamese army uniforms thirty years after the war ended and mourn the loss of their homeland, and pro-Palestine and pro-Israel demonstrators are in a never-ending row—diversity has gone into hyperspace in a region where multiculturalism is already considered passé.

This, after all, is the age of "hybridity," as coined by G. Pascal Zachary, in which individuals claim multiple memberships. Children born from so much intermixing have coined new words to describe themselves—Blaxicans, Hindjews, Chirish, Afropinos, Caureans, Japoricans, Cambofricans, Chungarians, Zebras, and Rainbows—coinages that confound the standard categories offered by the U.S. Census. What to do indeed when the category of "Other" threatens to be as large as anything like "Black" or "Hispanic" or "Asian"? At UC Berkeley, the authors remind us, nearly a quarter of students polled in 2004 identified themselves as "multi-racial or multi-ethnic."

But here is where extreme individualism cohabits with estranged communalism, often within the same block. Tightly knit tribes—Little Saigons, Chinatowns, Little Kabul—with their own in-language media and temples and churches, exist alongside Latino Muslims, black Buddhists, Mien teenagers speaking Ebonics. Cities meld into one another here, where neighborhoods overlap, and where every system—community, company, individual—is opened by various degrees and communicating with every other, constantly readjusting itself in many marvelous and surprising ways.

Under the Dragon therefore refutes easy framing. Take the sign that was on Oakland's Sun Hop Fat #1 Supermarket, a few blocks south of Lake Merritt on East 12th Street, until it burned down in 2006. It said, "American-Mexican-Chinese-Vietnamese-Thailand-Cambodia-Laos-Filipino-Oriental Food." Is this a symbol of a multicultural mess? Or could we all enter the place proudly, pretending the sign was hanging high over the global village gate?

Many of the photos and stories in this book are of what I call California moments, events in which something astonishing and marvelous in the experiment of cohabitation in California is revealed. Examples abound: an African devotee of Krishna praying to the sky; a Filipina playing the role of the Hindu goddess Lakshmi; Jesse Graham, the white preacher at the African American Mount Zion Baptist Church in West Berkeley, whose preaching moves spirits; and my favorite story, the Iranian psychotherapist who finds roots in America by attending to Cambodian refugees—a novel in the making.

Yet if the center does not hold, or rather, if we now live in a multi-centered reality, where not just society but individuals themselves have become diverse, with multiple affiliations and memberships, then what possible metaphor can capture it all?

The authors came up with one: under the flap of the dancing Chinese dragon at the Chinese New Year parade, Latinos and Russian immigrants and Samoans are found dancing along with the Chinese. It is both an apt and poetic image of this new undiscovered country.

But be warned: the horizontal metropolis is not seeking equilibrium. And, like the undulating dragon, it seeks to create new patterns and points of connection in a world that is constantly changing. No one book is therefore enough to capture the enormous complexity of our time.

One should admire these photos and stories, and see them as snapshots of an unabridged epic still waiting to be told. One should also applaud the authors' unwavering curiosity as they navigate the neighborhoods and streets and various communities of the Bay Area. See them, if you will, as postmodern Lewis and Clark, whose topography may yet lead us to the cosmopolitan frontier.

CHINESE NEW YEAR, SAN FRANCISCO. A TWO-HUNDRED-FOOT-LONG GOLDEN dragon snaked through the city's streets, held aloft by a hundred dancing men and women. The air thickened with acrid black smoke, and the deafening percussion of six hundred thousand firecrackers echoed along Chinatown's alleys and through the canyons of high-rise office buildings. Crowds filled the sidewalks six-deep. It was an energetic, joyous, dazzling scene— and yet somehow we felt unsatisfied.

For months, we had been combing the cities, small towns, and suburbs of the Bay Area in an effort to understand and document its booming multicultural mix. In the first decade of the new century, the region was gathering itself into a new assembly of cultures in which the influence of Asia, Latin America, the Caribbean, and other disparate parts of the world were greatly magnified. But for all its color and verve, the Chinese New Year parade seemed too familiar and predictable to illuminate the changes taking place in our midst—a stock image and story straight out of the slick magazines, tourist books, and TV news. Then a sudden cloudburst struck, and the gyrating dragon provided the only refuge. Under its hide, alongside the dancers, was an image of the more complicated and contradictory story we had been searching for.

The dragon was carried through the streets by young people from Chinatown, of course. But along with them were Latinos from the Mission District, immigrant Russians from the Richmond, Samoans from South San Francisco: an unlikely alliance of people who had quietly joined a ritual radically unrelated to their own backgrounds. In the process, they were covertly changing themselves in small, but important ways—even as they were forging a new Bay Area.

Kincaid Toy, who stood at the center of the dragon, puzzled out the mix. "My parents were very traditional Chinese," he said later, after he had finished helping one hundred other runners twist and turn the dragon up the hills of San Francisco. "Even though my father was the third generation here, he sent for my mother as a mail-order bride from China. But my wife is Irish, Danish, Swiss, and Italian. We live in suburbia and my kids know only 'thank you' in Chinese. But they go with me to this parade, and under the dragon I'm Chinese again. Well, not *Chinese* Chinese. My cultural connection is to Chinatown. To San Francisco, not China."

Kincaid Toy, Dragon Runner

It would be tempting at this point to appropriate this image and demand from the particulars of the story a grand and sweeping declaration about its larger social and historical meaning: *The future of us all lies under the dragon…* In many ways, it does. But the intermixing taking place under the dragon's hide only expresses part of the truth. Activities taking place in another Bay Area neighborhood soon provided a stark reminder of the rest.

IN THE CITY OF SUNNYVALE, WITHIN COMMUTING RANGE ON THE PENINSULA TO Silicon Valley, two local teams were in the midst of a hotly contested game of cricket. During one of the game's characteristic lulls, an onlooker pointed out that "cricket is like a religion in India." He might have added that it enjoyed a similar status in parts of Sunnyvale, where Indians now make up 10 percent of the population. To the immense satisfaction of many local enthusiasts, the city of Sunnyvale had constructed a municipal cricket pitch whose excellent design was commended by players and fans as far away as New Delhi and Bombay. It appeared that even in the midst of Sunnyvale's orderly tract homes, the very symbol of suburbia's bland homogeneity, the new mix of people was bringing forth lively, congenial changes to the status quo that were being met with official sanction and even a degree of public enthusiasm.

Later that afternoon, Vaishnavi Sridhar, a native of India, graciously opened the door to her home in nearby Cupertino and launched into a conversation that suggested a very different reality.

"I feel very cut off from the mainstream," declared Vaishnavi. "My interaction with other people is minimal and it's only other Indians that I know." Vaishnavi's alienation from her surroundings was not the result of language difficulties or an impenetrably foreign culture. "I have a master's degree in English literature," she said. "I wrote my thesis on Jane Austen. My grandfather would read us Byron and the Mahabarata side by side." Nevertheless, Vaishnavi had not cultivated any friends in Cupertino beyond her own ethnic circle. "Since I have come here," she admitted, "I haven't talked to any of my neighbors for more than a few minutes at a time. There are Caucasians and Chinese living around us, but we don't see much of them. I've had long conversations with a maximum of ten Caucasians in the ten years that I've lived here."

E pluribus unum. From many, one—some of the time…

We blend, intermingle, amalgamate, and forge ourselves into unexpected alloys. Yet at the same time, we isolate ourselves in enclaves of the familiar, protect privilege, and struggle preposterously to resist change. It all happens at once, making America a messy place, with the Bay Area ranking among its most gloriously disordered corners.

Under the dragon's skin, both truths prevail.

FESTIVAL OF INDIA, Fremont

Officer William Carattini and Karamjit "Ricky" Singh, who is Sikh

Officer William Carattini: "The photograph shows that the police department of Fremont welcomes the Muslim or the Hindu people. Ricky's been a real good friend of mine for years now. I met him when he was a clerk at a store on my beat. Knowing the different cultures makes me aware there are people who are different than most people here in America—the Catholic, Protestants, or whatever—and you can still be friends. We don't talk about religious beliefs—I respect he's Sikh or Hindu or Muslim, and he respects my religion."

Karamjit Singh—who immigrated to the United States from the Punjab twelve years ago: "Officer Carattini, he's my good buddy, and I think he's a little interested about my culture, too. I don't wear the turban and beard anymore because since 9/11 a lot of Sikh people get attacked. I'm working at a gas station and I don't want anything to happen to me. Be sure to put my other name beside the picture, too. It's Ricky."

DIWALI—INDIA'S FESTIVAL OF LIGHT, San Francisco
Sister Elizabeth decorates the Brahma Kumaris center

As the shortest days approach, India embarks on Diwali: "In the Bay Area we're from all nationalities, so Diwali here is our Western take on a very old Hindu holiday," says Sister Mary Friedland, of German heritage, raised Catholic near Chicago and converted to Hinduism. "Our day is spent transforming an American house into an Indian palace. The Festival of Lights is like Christmas, New Year's, and Chanukah for Indians."

Of the ten brothers and sisters living at the Brahma Kumaris center in San Francisco (including those of German, Hispanic, French, Filipino, Japanese, African, and Indian heritage), three were raised Catholic, one Lutheran, one Quaker, one Buddhist, and four Hindu (from India and Africa).

The making of the goddess Lakshmi

During Diwali, Hindus pay homage to Lakshmi, the four-armed Goddess of Wealth, to bring them prosperity in the coming year. In San Francisco, Sister Gwen Torres, a Filipina, becomes Lakshmi.

BLACK NATIVE AMERICANS, Berkeley
Don Little Cloud Davenport

*Don Little Cloud Davenport is a founder of the Black Native American Association: "My grandfather was
Chickasaw and African American from Sudan. Seminole tribal leaders accepted him to live among them,
and he sired two sets of children on the Crow Creek Reservation in Florida. My mother is Seminole/Creek/
Chickasaw and African American. I am Seminole with Muskogee/Creek/Chickasaw and African ancestry.
I am of the Bird Clan, and a direct descendant of the Ancient Nubian Empire, born in Jackson, Michigan,
on a route of the Underground Railroad where slaves fled to Canada."*

John Beautiful Sage and Peggy Royster

*John Beautiful Sage's paternal family is from North Africa; his mother's family is Siskiyou and
Canadian Blackfoot.*

*"I grew up Catholic, so I didn't know anything about my Native American background, hardly knew I
had it. My mom didn't do the culture thing at all. I got involved in things I'm not proud to tell you about.
Then I got into a drug addiction recovery program. I was real sick, and some people from the Native American Health Center came over to the program. They saved me. I was ashamed of myself, but I stood up and
faced the sky and asked the creator for help. The spirit—God, the all living, the grandmother and grandfather of the earth, he of infinite wonders—came to rescue me, and I'm an upstanding citizen now. The spirit
of my ancestors helped me see my true colors."*

CARIJAMA CARIBBEAN CARNIVAL, Oakland
Trinidadian dance group Mas Makers Massive

Jackie Artman, from Trinidad, was one of the founders of Oakland's Carijama: "Carijama is short for Caribbeans Jamming. Everyone from any culture can participate. Carnival breaks barriers. I've never liked that word, 'minority.' It's a put-down. 'Minority' makes me feel lesser. California has more of what they call minorities, but what I see is some people get the big slice of the apple and people of color get the scraps. So Carijama is one place where we stand together in celebration—it doesn't matter the color of the skin, the ethnic background, the religion. In Carijama, from the babies to the older folks, we're all in the park celebrating. It's a beautiful feeling when I come to Carijama."

Virginia Denato, Islands of Fire dance troupe

Tomi Seon, Artistic Director of Islands of Fire: "Trinidad and Tobago were colonized by Britain, France, and Spain. Then when the slaves became free they wore costumes depicting the European dance balls, masks and big gowns. My ancestors had to fight for the right to wear those things, and now it's spread to Oakland and it's bringing the community together. Virginia Denato's an American, but she's been adopted as a Caribbean person."

DRAGON BOAT RACES, Oakland

Dragon boat racing originated in China over two thousand years ago. The race day traditionally opened with a Taoist ceremony of "awakening the dragons." Twenty paddlers synchronized their strokes by following the beat of drummers in fifty-foot-long boats decorated with dragon heads and tails.

Opposite: *Monks from a local Thai Buddhist temple were asked to bless the Chinese dragon boats. The Venerable Manat Suksa-Ad presided, and observed: "Boat racing is Chinese—not Thai. And the Chinese people, they put the fruit on our table. Thai culture just puts the flower. They asked me to pour holy water in the boat so the boat will be the winner. This is not Buddhism. We don't stay to see who wins—but we are happy to be here and make the good luck for them. The practice of Buddhism even in Thailand was never pure. We adapt."*

    Caught up in the excitement, the Thai monks did stay to watch the race.

WHAT IS IT LIKE TO LIVE IN THE BAY AREA TODAY, AS THE REGION coalesces into one of history's most heterogeneous multiethnic societies?

The old metaphors fail us. The early twentieth-century ideal of the melting pot seems brutal, crude, and distinctly unrealistic, with its emphasis on scouring away cultural distinctions and sacrificing individual identity to the formation of a standard national type. New metaphors that liken America to a kaleidoscope, a mosaic, a salad bowl, or even a heaping plate of cultural chop suey simply sound preposterous and strained, with a self-conscious, sanitized idealization of difference. "Diversity" and "multiculturalism," with their ring of shopworn convenience, have been rendered practically meaningless by overuse and imprecision.

Of course, our streets have for decades resounded with the speech of a wider world—the cadences of Mexico echoing amid the less familiar accents of Guatemala and Peru; the century-old prevalence of mainland Cantonese accommodating new voices from Hong Kong and Taiwan, as well as newcomers conversing in Vietnamese, Khmer, and Thai—along with Tagalog, Tamil, Telugu, Turkish, and more than one hundred other languages. But today, if you listen carefully, you will also hear an unprecedented intermingling of tongues—the first sign that something new is taking shape on our city streets and suburbs.

GATHER AROUND THE SATURDAY AFTERNOON BARBECUE PIT AT THE ZAYTUNA Institute, an islamic study center in downtown Hayward, and you'll find students taking a break from their beginning Arabic class to share a Mexican *asada* and converse in their native tongue, Spanish. The meal's two cooks, Daniel Denton and Walter Gomez, emigrated from Mexico and El Salvador, and then converted from Catholicism to Islam. Join the crowd of American Buddhists in downtown Oakland filling three thousand seats at the Paramount Theater and listen to the resonant thrum of the Japanese chant—*Nam Myoho Renge Kyo*—and you will notice that at least half the faces in the auditorium are black. Slip into a pew at the African American Mount Zion Baptist Church in West Berkeley, and if you can look beyond the impassioned gestures and rhythmic intonations of the young preacher, Jesse Graham, it will gradually dawn upon you that he is white. Stand at the foot of the bandstand in San

Oakland's Fruitvale District

Francisco's Stern Grove, and you will see the crowd of elderly Chinese men nodding to one another in mute approval as Anthony Brown's Asian American Orchestra concludes its premiere of *American Rhapsodies*—a recomposition of George Gershwin's *Rhapsody in Blue* that substitutes a pair of Chinese hammered dulcimers for the traditional piano and sends the sound and spirit of the music sprawling across influences from the Russian *shtetl* and Tin Pan Alley to the Mississippi Delta and the Japanese imperial court.

The Bay Area today is a place where people come together, often inadvertently, to confound narrow expectations about race and culture. In a huge Victorian mansion in San Francisco's Haight-Ashbury district, the young woman portraying the role of Lakshmi—the four-armed goddess central to the Hindu celebration of Diwali—is Gwen Torres, a Filipina. In Fremont, the Bay Area's fourth largest city, a small strip of the Centerville district is famously, if informally, known as Little Kabul. Here the teenagers propped up against a lowered GTO and decked out in Mexican *cholo* style, with sagging jeans and woolen Pendletons hanging open over their white t-shirts, speak to one another not in Spanish or English or even Spanglish—but in the Pashtu of Afghanistan. A few miles away, at the Naz 8 Cinema (which bills itself as "North America's First Multicultural Entertainment Megaplex," screening films from India, Pakistan, China, Korea, the Philippines, and Afghanistan), it is the fare at the snack bar, or "*chaat* corner," that suggests the reshuffled mix of the world outside: veggie samosas, veggie kabob, veggie pizza, veggie burritos, egg rolls, and nachos—with mango, baby coconut, and lychee ice creams for dessert.

The jumble and miscellany that characterize the Bay Area today are best viewed by roving along the boundaries where people encounter one another—points of merging and resistance, upheaval and accommodation, blend and distinction. The sum of these interactions would seem to require a new metaphor—a successor to the ridiculous salad bowl and the sentimental mosaic. Yet nothing quite seems apt. The changes taking place are too contradictory, particular, and squirming with life to be contained within a single image. Our society's appetite for change is too pervasive, insatiable, even cannibalistic to be reduced to a stock phrase. Ethnicity, nationality, culture, and religion persistently intersect, overlap, startle, and confuse. The Bay Area has leapt out of the melting pot and into the fire—where the new America is being forged.

IRANIAN NOROOZ, Berkeley

At the vernal equinox each year, Persians jump over a bonfire to cleanse their spirits while chanting an ancient verse in Farsi: "I give my yellowness to you. I will take your redness." In Berkeley, cultures clashed: the fire department insisted that Persians substitute Duraflame® logs for bonfires. Persians have celebrated Norooz, based on the "universal struggle between dark and light," since the times of Zoroaster (600 B.C.).

JESSE, WHAT ARE YOU?

HEADS NODDED, HANDS CLAPPED, AND SEVERAL MEMBERS OF THE CONGREGATION CHUCKLED IN recognition. Jesse Graham, the young white preacher, he was good. Jesse preached the truth up on that podium. He was a white boy, no way around that, but he had the gift and anybody with eyes and ears had to admit it was true.

Even Reverend Thompson, the pastor at Mount Zion Baptist Church, agreed that Jesse had a calling, and he said so publicly. Jesse had just turned twenty-three years old, and the pastor was helping to cultivate his talent, guiding him. Reverend Thompson liked to compare himself to Jesse's corner man—a boxer's ringside coach charged with whispering into his ear the necessary advice and inspiration before flinging him back into the fray. Sometimes he even called Jesse his son, meaning his spiritual son. A black minister amid his all-black congregation: Reverend Thompson would suppress a mischievous grin and slyly point to Jesse, declaring, "Yes, that is my son. I am his father."

"So the holy spirit went forth and opened the mind of the Prodigal Son," Jesse cried out from the podium, and the men and women in the pews muttered their approval. "And the Prodigal Son came to himself!"

Reverend Thompson had never met anyone who could absorb the lessons of the gospel like Jesse. No convert of any skin color or class background had demonstrated an equivalent zeal to live in the spirit. Yet Jesse was struggling this morning, striving to reach the emotional peak of his sermon. Reverend Thompson could see that Jesse was climbing a steep mountain, and he needed a hand.

Jesse closed his eyes and rocked, slightly out of time, his head bobbing, the rhythm jagged, and then he stared straight up at the ceiling, shifting his weight from foot to foot.

Reverend Thompson moved up closer behind him.

"Who are you?" the young white preacher asked the black congregation—echoing the fundamental question that he had been demanding of himself all his life. "Ask the holy spirit to help you come back to your true nature, who you really are!" Jesse squeezed shut his eyes, stanching tears. His voice dropped to a whisper. "Look at the man in the mirror..."

IN EIGHTH GRADE, JESSE GATHERED TOGETHER HIS FRIENDS, ALL OF THEM BLACK, AND HE ANNOUNCED that he would no longer tolerate his nickname.

Jesse Graham and congregation, Berkeley

"Don't call me 'White Boy,'" ordered Jesse. "Not ever again."

Jesse's parents, both white, had named him after Jesse Jackson, whom they had admired for years. But after they divorced, and Jesse moved with his mother and brother from their tract home in suburban Fremont to Oakland's inner city—where almost all his classmates were black and poor, and middle class kids of any race were seldom seen—the origin of Jesse's name was the last topic he wanted to bring up for discussion. Instead, he kept his mouth shut, and he studied the balance of power played out each day in the school yard. He sharpened his skills for survival.

One afternoon, Jesse fought one of the few other white students in school—a tough kid who prided himself on hanging with the toughest black kids. As they scrambled in the dirt, limbs locked, spinning circles like an insanely busted compass, the other kids on the sidelines were forced to take stock. Jesse Graham was earning himself a reputation: he's that crazy badass white boy.

"It's like I had to grow teeth and claws," explained Jesse. "I had to know who I was and figure how I was going to play it out. I adapted to my environment. And it made me grow."

With time, Jesse also understood why his presence in the classroom and on the streets of Oakland might provoke resentment.

"How come you didn't go with your cousins to private school?" a black kid challenged him. "You're stuck with us, huh? Now, how do we feel about you?"

Jesse pretended to be mixed-race. His hair was black and wavy, almost crinkly, and his complexion was dark, perhaps Mediterranean or Eastern European. Conceivably, there could have been a black ancestor lodged somewhere in his family's past—just as many of his lighter-skinned African American friends were undoubtedly the descendants of a white man lurking someplace in their own mix. But this question of skin color, of origins, and therefore, allegiances, was never settled for Jesse.

"In my school," Jesse recalled, "black people were the dominant race and white people got picked on. White people weren't strong—you could bully them. Everybody's racist against you, targeting you because you're white. You usually hear the opposite, but that's not what it's like."

Yet with an expanding group of black friends at his side, Jesse no longer felt like an outsider, a victim. "I learned that there's positions of power," Jesse explained, "like who's up, who's down, who's in the middle? Who can be confronted and who can't. It'd be an awesome college course in cultural dynamics," he said, "but this is something I had to learn when I was nine."

When a carload of Filipino kids from another neighborhood showed up one afternoon at school wearing sunglasses and visors with gang initials tattooed across the brims, Jesse immediately joined a swarm of black kids who mobbed them, beat them to the ground, and kicked them again and again until the strangers piled back in their cars and retreated to safety.

Jesse was heading straight into the kinds of trouble that swallow up countless young men on the streets of Oakland. "If I had grown up in a white community," he admitted, "I might have joined the Aryan Brotherhood or a motorcycle gang. When you're in pain, you reach out to the people nearby who are doing bad things—and there's some of that in every culture." Proximity is destiny: Jesse fashioned himself after the thugs in his midst.

Luckily, around this time, Jesse also discovered the first great redeeming passion of his life.

JESSE STARTED WITH PICK-UP GAMES AT THE NEIGHBORHOOD BASKETBALL COURT, EVERYBODY WORKING their moves like miniature impersonations of Bill Russell, Gary Payton, and Jason Kidd, stars of the NBA who had all come up playing ball in Oakland. Jesse played every day with his crew and when a new player, invariably black, showed up on the court and introduced himself to the others by slamming the white boy ass backwards into the pole, the rest of the team quickly rallied around.

"Do that again," Jesse's friends growled at the newcomer, "you gonna get hurt."

At Oakland Tech, Jesse earned a place on the team. Five thousand fans crowding the gymnasium, with Jesse Graham the only white player on the court—the only white face in the entire league. That's Jesse out there, pivoting mid-court to face the stands and mock the crowd, his long white legs and arms

Facing page: *Mount Zion Baptist Church*

33

dangling provocatively out from his satin shorts and jersey. "I was the smart-mouth tough white kid," he remembered, "that forty people wanted to beat up afterwards." And although Jesse looked like an outsider, he played like he belonged.

"What really caught my eye at first," recalled David Manson, Jesse's coach for the competitive summer league, "was the flavor of Jesse's game. He'd picked up the flashy urban style of play that's intended to intimidate and dominate your opponent." Manson easily set aside the chief distinguishing characteristic of his new player: the glaring fact of his whiteness. "Jesse had a very urbanized, very inner-city, African American sense of who he was," said Manson. "You saw it in his expressions, his gestures. Unconsciously," admitted Manson, "I treated him as though he had the same needs, the same developmental challenges, as the African American kids."

At the heart of Manson's dedication to Jesse and the other players on his team was his own religious commitment—an involvement in a wing of the black Baptist church that stressed works as emphatically as faith. Occasionally, Manson dragged his players along to services at his church, Mount Zion Baptist in West Berkeley. For many of the young men, the church felt familiar, homey, comforting—their grandmother's old-time religion; the price you had to pay now and then to play ball. Jesse had shown up once or twice along with the rest of the team, the only white boy in the pews.

"Life coach" was how Manson thought of himself—the term evoking both his area of concern and the duration of his own commitment to his players. Manson disciplined his kids and he pressed down particularly hard on Jesse. "You go home," he ordered, "and study as hard as you play ball! You get in trouble and you'll find yourself off this team! Now look into my eyes when I'm talking to you, because God damn it, you better understand that I love you!"

NBA dreams...Jesse had them, along with all the other guys on the team. And one tool for turning those dreams into possibilities was Future Stars basketball camp in Charlottesville, Virginia. Future Stars pitted the best young athletes in the country against one another under the eyes of scouts from prestigious universities that Manson's kids otherwise had no chance of entering. Jesse wanted desperately to attend.

"Leave that crazy white boy home," Manson's assistant coach had advised. These words now passed through Manson's mind, accompanied by a wave of nausea as he stood in the Baltimore airport, halfway to basketball camp, explaining to the sergeant that Yes, he was personally responsible for Jesse Graham.

"See," stammered Jesse, handcuffed and staring down at the floor, "there was this girl I took into the bathroom and then..."

Manson cut him short. The airport cops could feel the heat rising off the coach. They surrendered the troublesome white teenager into the black man's hands.

"And then somebody else walked in the bathroom," Jesse explained desperately, "and she saw what we were doing, and she started screaming..."

And that's when Jesse took off.

He had sprinted down the corridor, bounding over a barrier of suitcases, almost smashing into a clot of passengers whisking their children out of harm's way. He burst through a door reading NO EXIT and the alarms rang madly until the airport police caught him, pinned his arms at the elbows, and hustled him down the corridor as several hundred people gawked and hooted and shook their heads at the spectacle.

Manson now marched Jesse to the ticket counter and paid for the return trip to Oakland with his own cash. He stood at the gate as Jesse boarded his flight, waiting for the plane to lift off. But it didn't even taxi. Five minutes later, Jesse was pacing back across the blacktop, escorted by four flight attendants.

Jesse had threatened that if the plane took off, he would open the door mid-flight and kill everybody on board.

That night in jail, waiting for his father to arrive from California and take him home, Jesse curled himself up in a ball on the cell's floor, and he wailed and hollered and beat the floor with his fists. "Then

I looked up at the ceiling and I screamed at God: 'Why? Why do I have so much pain, it's tearing my heart. Why?"

FOR MOST OF HIS ADOLESCENCE, JESSE HAD BEEN AN ATHLETE, A WHITE BASKETBALL PLAYER IN A black world, with sufficient skills, dedication, and guts to be taken seriously on and off the court. Now he wasn't even a member of the team. He was nobody, just as he had been at nine years of age— a scared, strange little white boy sticking out where he did not belong.

Jesse quit school, left home, lived for weeks in a one-bedroom East Oakland apartment with his closest friend and his mother and three other children. "Jesse, there are two worlds out there," she told him. "The streets and the white man's world. You know the streets, but you don't know nothing about the white man's world." Jesse had no idea where he belonged.

One night, nodding along miserably to Tupac rapping on the CD player about life's incessant pain, Jesse drew a warm bath, lit some candles, and turned the lights down low. Before submerging himself in the bath water, he addressed the family video camera: "Mom, I love you. Good-bye." And then he swallowed nineteen pills. Three hours later, Jesse was still sitting in the bathtub, the water cold, his head numb and buzzy, just waking to the fact that he was still ridiculously alive.

That's when Jesse first heard God speaking to him. "I remember every word. He said, 'It's not your time yet. I have something for you to do.'"

Jesse hopped in his car and streaked across town. When he burst through the front doors of Mount Zion Baptist Church, Manson was standing at the pulpit, preaching to the congregation. Two hundred black faces turned to watch the white boy scramble to a seat, his face full of wild hope and terror.

Jesse was surprised to find several of his former teammates sitting in the pews. He slid in between them, pressed up shoulder to shoulder.

The Reverend Mike Thompson, Mount Zion Baptist Church's pastor, stood at the pulpit. "The true measure of a man," he roared to the congregation, swaying in place, his big fist pummeling the air, "the way we first size up and then finally judge a man is not by his age or his profession, his wealth or his position, his background or race or the shade of his skin—certainly not by that. It's by the strength of his belief. Belief in what he feels, what boils up from his guts."

Jesse couldn't take his eyes off Reverend Thompson—who stood six feet five and weighed three hundred pounds. A gangbanger in his youth, a survivor from the streets: Jesse was certain the pastor was talking directly to him.

Jesse collapsed into tears. The guys on the team watched: Jesse Graham, Crazy Badass White Dude, crumpled up beside them in church, bleeding tears.

Manson led his players to a quiet room in the back of the church and they prayed for Jesse as he screeched and babbled—embarrassed, shocked, and elated.

"I AM HERE TO PREACH TO YOU TODAY," JESSE DECLAIMED, "ABOUT THE PRODIGAL SON." HE ROCKED SLOW and steady at the pulpit at Mount Zion Baptist Church. On edge, a bit fearful. Like before a game.

And from the pews echoed encouragement: "Yeah, yeah! Yes, you are!"

When Jesse first telephoned Reverend Thompson one Sunday afternoon some two years after his breakdown in church and told him that he believed God had called upon him to preach, his pastor responded curtly: "It's about time. We've been waiting for you." The drugs, fights, suicide attempts, the craziness—that was all in the past, part of his testimony now. Nothing to be proud of. But people understood. His people.

"When Jesus came down to Earth," Jesse told the congregation, "he chose to hang around the prostitutes, the drug dealers, the convicts, the backsliders—these rejected-by-society people, like you and me." A foolish mistake. Jesse's eyes rolled up to the ceiling. "Uh, like me. Excuse me."

Hands clapped, the congregation laughed, excusing him. He was young, still learning.

Mount Zion Baptist Church

"Like me, a person who has a jail record, and addictions under his belt, who hasn't made it in society. Something about Jesus draws us sinners to him…"

Jesse turned from the pulpit to face Reverend Thompson. He latched onto the pastor's huge wrist and drew him several feet across the altar—the Reverend serving as a cooperative prop, amused, quietly beaming. It was impossible to tell if the move was planned or improvised. Jesse hardly glanced at his sermon, though he had written page after page of complete paragraphs, the key points marked in yellow highlighter. Instead, the words flooded out of his mouth. It was like being in the zone on the basketball court, playing better than he could play; preaching beyond himself.

Reverend Thompson stood directly behind Jesse and lifted his hands above his own huge shoulders.

"If you're caught up in the streets," declaimed Jesse, struggling to gather momentum, "that's not you. If you're caught up in the gangs, that's not you. You come to yourself!"

Just a few months earlier, in the company of Reverend Thompson, Jesse had met Jesse Jackson, heard him preach, even shook his hand. "He talked about our heritage as black people," Jesse later told a friend, catching himself on the "our"—laughing at himself.

"I remember the day when I met Jesus Christ," declared Jesse, pushing ahead with his sermon. "Right over there." His index finger darted out at the middle pews. "And God didn't say, 'Jesse, why did you smoke cocaine?' He didn't say, 'Jesse, why did you become an alcoholic?' He didn't say, 'Jesse, I saw you with those women, and what you did was wrong!'"

Reverend Thompson lifted his hands above Jesse's head, his enormous palms waving, his great bulk sheltering the younger man. "Yes, yes, yes," said Reverend Thompson. Just a little further, he was urging Jesse on, coaxing him up to that mountaintop. Insisting that Jesse come to himself among the people who had shared his pain and mistakes, and now served as the inspiration and witness to his present reclamation.

Not too many like him, thought Reverend Thompson—our Jesse Graham. Our Jesse.

The organ blared, cymbals crashed, the bass drum thudded the floor like a frantic heartbeat. The choir broke into praise song, hands clapping—"There Ain't Nobody Loves Me Like Jesus."

Jesse raised up both arms above his head and shouted to the congregation: "God told me: Jesse, I accept you as my son!"

INDIA INDEPENDENCE DAY, Fremont

Lal Singh Bhatti, master of Indian classical music and "king of the dhol" (an Indian drum), came to Fremont from the Punjab, India: "I always smile, because the bhangra *is the Punjabi dance of joy. I teach my students, the smile is part of the dance. August 15th celebrates India's freedom from the British. On this day, Hindu people, Sikh people, Muslim people, we are all Indians. In the Punjab, we light bonfires and celebrate the glory—like your 4th of July.*

"Those boys, you can see they are not my students, because their fingers don't point to the air, they don't wear turbans, and they don't smile. They're just jumping up and down, not dancing the Punjabi bhangra. *And no, no, no, their clothes are all modernized. Those boys cannot be Indians from Fremont. They must be from Union City."*

Patti Kim, San Francisco

MR. AND MISS GAY ASIAN PACIFIC ALLIANCE PAGEANT, San Francisco
Minh Ta

Minh Ta came to the United States from Vietnam in 1985: "In the world of transgender and drag, you have to be outlandish and extravagant. But those aren't ideal qualities for Vietnamese women, who have an elegant, delicate beauty—a little timid, with sensuality and mystery. People think beauty pageant winners are always Filipinos, that Vietnamese don't look good. I want them to know there are Vietnamese with lovely features like mine."

PURIM, CHABAD OF THE EAST BAY, Berkeley
Rabbi Chanan Feld (soccer coach, accountant, tent designer), Elior Vas (psychiatrist), Yehudah Landsman (college student), Yakov Nurik (lawyer)

Rabbi Yehudah Ferris, Director of Berkeley Chabad—a group of Chassidic Jews that dates back to the town of Lubavitch, in Russia: "Why the Mexican hat? It's Purim! God concealed his face when the Jews were almost annihilated by our archenemy Haman. So we wear disguises, we push the envelope, we question assumptions—to show that we're all equal before God. One guy looks like a Mexican and the others look like old European rabbis—which is what they look like every day, not just for Purim. Is this distinctly Bay Area? No. It transcends time and place and geographic borders. Could this be Eastern Europe? Yes. Anywhere. Because there are no more boundaries. And that's a good thing."

WEDGED BETWEEN OAKLAND AND BERKELEY AT A SNARL OF FREEWAY winding toward the Bay Bridge—set off in an obscure corner of the Bay Street shopping center in the small city of Emeryville—you will find a peculiar reminder of the Bay Area's oldest settlement.

At first glance, it merely looks like a bit of odd landscaping—a single, man-made, twenty-foot-high hill bristling with wild clumps of native grasses. But according to a row of shoulder-high granite tablets flanking the hill, each etched with dates and corresponding information about the native people who first lived along the shoreline, the hill turns out to be a monument—a diminutive recreation of a huge shellmound that once stood on these grounds.

Some twenty-eight hundred years ago, ancestors of the Ohlone Indians began piling the remains of shellfish and other animals discarded from the millions of meals consumed in their village. The mound grew steadily, and eventually the tribe also began using it as a communal burial site. Then, four hundred years ago, the settlement dispersed, leaving as evidence of the Native Americans' prolonged stay a steep hill of rich, highly organic soil rising sixty feet in the air.

Today no sign exists of the original Emeryville shellmound and burial site. In the late nineteenth century, it was leveled to construct the Blue Star Pavilion, one of the East Bay's most luxurious ballrooms and the centerpiece of the popular Shellmound Park. The park was completely dismantled by the mid-twentieth century, and the shoreline fronting the former village site was covered with paint and pesticide factories, a machine shop and trucking facility, and a battery of ruptured storage tanks leaking lead, arsenic, and hydrogen sulfide into the soil and out into the bay.

The sole reminder of this history is the storefront monument.

Most shoppers pass by without notice. The miniature shellmound replica lies outside the store grid and beyond the massive blocks of concrete parking lots. Security guards and store clerks express confusion about its location or register surprise about its very existence. Occasionally, the odd clutch of shoppers will blunder upon it as they stray from the commercial maze, and they read the granite chronology with expressions of incredulity and then alarm.

Aztec dancer and friend, Mission District, San Francisco

Unmentioned is the fact that prior to the shopping center's construction, the remains of over one thousand native people were disinterred from the spot where the shellmound once stood. Excavation crews stumbled upon the skeletal poses of women laid to rest with babies, adults twined together with interlocking limbs, bodies assembled in groups. Yet, though this grisly disturbance of the dead is not mentioned, the very existence of the shellmound monument hints at human vulnerability and transience. The display speaks to the ease with which whole settlements, even peoples, not only can be, but inevitably will be, erased by time. We walk, eat, sleep, and now even shop upon bones of the dead.

The shellmound took two thousand years to erect. Within a hundred years of European settlement in the Bay Area, it was capped, topped, slashed, and obliterated. Now we can view the first strata of local life only through symbolic representation and by force of imagination—while descendants of the Bay Area's earliest inhabitants strain to sort out their own lineage.

IN OAKLAND, THE UPTOWN REDEVELOPMENT PROJECT AIMS TO REVITALIZE A NINE-block stretch between San Pablo and Telegraph Avenues—an area characterized for decades by empty streets and crumbling buildings. With the construction of over thirteen hundred new housing units, stores, parking, and a small public square, Uptown hopes to draw residents and businesses back into the city. Yet only after the project was ready to launch did it become clear that more than one hundred and thirty years ago, a nearly forgotten Chinatown thrived in its midst.

Starting in 1867, many of Oakland's Chinese, who had originally flocked to California to help build the transcontinental railroad, settled into a block-long enclave between 19th and 20th Streets on San Pablo Avenue. The hundred or so residents of the old San Pablo Chinatown—one of several once scattered throughout Oakland—worked as fishermen and shrimpers, cooks and waiters, barbers, tailors, and storekeepers. The streets bustled with life, the wheels of commerce driving the neighborhood from dawn to dark.

"We call these places Chinatowns," cautioned Anna Naruta, an archaeologist who has studied the area's early census records, "but the reality was more complicated. They were also mixed neighborhoods with Chinese and non-Chinese residents in the same area. It was like today with people mixing it up together. You go house by house, and you discover guys from Mexico, Prussia, Norway. Some rooming houses had Irish and Chinese living together. It's an amazingly diverse time," insisted Naruta. "Unfortunately, the conventional histories of how people settled the Bay Area were usually written by Anglo boosters tying everything back to Europe. We lost a lot."

Indeed, when local entrepreneurs planned a business corridor slicing through the neighborhood and connecting to the new City Hall on 14th Street, they identified the primary obstacle as the Chinese. An 1875 issue of the *Oakland Tribune* railed against the San Pablo Chinatown, insisting that "this 'settlement' seems like a plague spot in the midst of paradise." The reporter went on to denounce the area's "blight" and advocated tearing down the wooden structures and driving out the Chinese residents.

The only sign of the district's early history that has lasted into the twenty-first century lies at the fringe of the Uptown project—a pair of flat-panel, wood-framed, two-story storefronts that most recently housed the tailors Hing Chong & Company. When the developers' bulldozers finally grind to a halt, and new buildings rise from the neighborhood's shattered ground to dramatically reshape the city center, no structures will remain to recall the dispersed Chinatown—much less render with clarity one of the key moments in Oakland's ongoing experiment in multiethnic living.

ONE GROUP BUILDS UPON THE REMAINS OF ANOTHER, AND THE PHYSICAL EVIDENCE of our communal history stands perpetually in jeopardy.

In San Francisco, the renovation of Peace Plaza, off Geary Street in the heart of Japantown, has gained substantial civic support and city funding over the past decade. But the effort has been driven primarily by *nisei*, the second-generation Japanese Americans now in their seventies and eighties. With the city's Japanese population remaining static over the past three decades, and younger people leaving the city for more affordable housing in the suburbs, the neighborhood now faces the prospect of one day turning into a kind of theme park of cultural remembrance—the uplift of pagoda roofs, the shoji sliding doors constructed of wood and rice paper, the *kansho-niwa* contemplation garden, koi ponds, and all the other architectural references to Japanese culture unrelated to the Korean store owners who have assumed a burgeoning share of local business, or to the black, white, and Latino children and teenagers who fill the streets. Indeed, as the Japanese population recedes, the neighborhood has grown more emphatically "Japanese" in physical detail and cultural thrust. One might frequent Japantown to attend a Japanese language class, learn to meditate, view an exhibit of artists commemorating Hiroshima and Nagasaki, shop at the Kintetsu Mall and Kinokuniya Bookstore, or help organize the annual Northern California Cherry Blossom Festival. Yet the Japanese population of the neighborhood is scarcely more than one thousand—a fifth of its former size. With time, Japantown may be Japanese only in name and lingering edifice.

Less than two miles away, housed in the former San Francisco Main Library, the Asian Art Museum of San Francisco has managed to twine together the present and past, if only by accident. Inside the newly renovated building, the visitor is struck first by the immensity of the museum's holdings—nearly fifteen thousand artifacts packed into three floors covering six thousand years of Asian history. The subtext is clear: Asia now represents one of the Bay Area's main cultural currents, and the museum's relocation from the outlying district of Golden Gate Park to the heart of the city confirms the Asian American community's size and influence. Yet the building's façade also suggests a strategic compromise between East and West. The old public library is a landmark building; alterations to its façade are prohibited. As a result, the Asian Art Museum has been compelled to retain the building's exterior stone scrolls, which are inscribed with the names of Plato, Dante, Shakespeare, Cervantes, Balzac, Emerson, Thoreau, and two dozen other luminaries of Western civilization. This roster of the key writers of Europe and America embossed upon the ramparts of a great treasure-house of Asian art suggests both the primacy of chance in the intermingling of cultures—and the slender hope that the cultivation of one tradition need not result in the erasure of another.

Al Shen, Chinatown, Oakland: "We wear Mexican hats because there are quite a bit of Spanish who also live here and we want to blend in."

Benh Nakajo, account manager with Japan Airlines, member of the Executive Committee of the Cherry Blossom Parade: "Look at the people walking around Japantown—all these Koreans, Chinese, Vietnamese who've come to the U.S., while the Japanese community grows smaller. We have few new immigrants to maintain our Japanese culture.

"The Cherry Blossom Parade is the only place third-, fourth-, and fifth-generation Japanese American kids get to see what being Japanese is. The woman in the photo with the kimono and such elegant hair—I want the kids to see how beautiful and interesting that traditional outfit is, with the clan markings and the ornaments in her hair. I want to tell the kids who are Japanese in name only, isn't that lady attractive? And her hair, isn't that something to be proud of?"

EDWARD AMERICANO AND THE AFGHAN GAS STATION ATTENDANT

IN HER CHAMBERS DURING A BREAK BEFORE THE AFTERNOON HEARINGS AT THE SUPERIOR COURT IN Hayward, Judge Peggy Hora marveled at how much detail she recalled from the case of Edward Americano, a nineteen-year-old Mexican American man accused of assaulting a gas station attendant from Afghanistan. For years, car thieves, muggers, wife beaters, and drug dealers had marched in a predictable procession in front of her bench. Few provided behavior worth remembering.

"I knew Eduardo was a thug," said the judge, using the Spanish pronunciation for his name, "but I also found him charming." She smiled awkwardly at the contradiction. "He was a good looking kid, not physically threatening, and he didn't do that gang posturing thing or give me those snotty looks I see in court every day." She leaned back in her black leather recliner. "Then, of course, there was the hate crime aspect. That always gets my attention."

While whites and Latinos had for years formed the majority of the small, blue-collar town of Hayward, more recent immigrants from Africa, India, the Middle East, and Southeast Asia had altered the ethnic landscape. During her years on the bench, Peggy Hora focused on understanding the styles and needs of the people from each culture that stood before her. "Cultural awareness around here is not just some politically correct horsepucky," she observed. "It's real."

The case of Edward Americano stuck in the judge's mind because she believed she had altered the defendant's prejudices and behavior. That was a rarity, she asserted, in any court.

Neither the prosecution nor the defense debated the facts of the case. Edward had pulled into a Hayward Exxon station. As he pumped gas, some spilled to the pavement. Edward demanded that the attendant, Saeed Zarakani, pay him back two dollars for the spillage. Saeed refused, blaming the young man's carelessness. "I know how to pump gas!" yelled Edward, and the argument rapidly escalated until he punched the attendant, knocked him to the ground, and kicked him in the head. When asked later about what happened, Edward didn't quibble. "We had a royal rumble going on."

Judge Hora had presided over hundreds of cases of pointless, stupid violence. But this incident shook her.

"What bothered me most about that fight," she said, "was that the Mexican American lad who beat the snot out of the Afghan attendant was shouting things like 'raghead' and 'go back where you came from.' I believe I was more distraught than the victim about the racist aspect of the crime. You don't go

Afghanistan refugee Arman Arif in his store, Fremont

calling Afghan people ragheads!" she declared. "And here's Eduardo, not two generations removed from Mexico." She threw up her hands in disgust. "There's always a hierarchy in racism."

Saeed testified that Edward had shouted "fucking Arab" during the fight. Edward denied this, and none of the witnesses at the scene recalled any hate speech.

Peggy Hora sentenced Edward to one hundred and eighty days in jail. Then she announced to the court, "I'm also concerned about the racial epithets that were thrown around in this case. So I'm instructing the district attorney to find a way to educate Mr. Americano about the Afghans, who are a large part of our South County community. He needs to know what the people in Afghanistan went through under the Soviets—that they are in this country as political refugees."

When the district attorney reported back to the judge, he relayed a new finding in the case. "I talked with Mr. Zarakani again," said the D.A. "He is not from Afghanistan. Mr. Zarakani is Persian. He's from Iran."

Judge Hora was stunned. "How did we mistake an Iranian for an Afghan all through the trial?" she asked. She had already contacted the director of the local Afghan Refugee Support Services, and he'd agreed to provide Edward with "a series of lectures on cultural diversity."

"Maybe we should all go," the judge told the D.A.

This case of mistaken ethnicity, Judge Hora later learned, had started with the police officer on the beat who filed the crime report as an assault against an Afghan man. The D.A., public defender, judge, and, of course, Edward Americano had simply extended the error, never asking Mr. Zarakani about his origins.

Judge Hora smiled as she recalled the end of the story. Rising from the chair in her chambers, she slid on her black robe and walked to the courtroom door. She was ready to ascend the bench for the afternoon cases.

"I'll never forget what Eduardo told me after he finished his jail term and time at the Afghan cultural center," reflected the judge. "He said, 'You know, the Afghan culture is five thousand years old!' His eyes lit up, he was filled with wonder. So even though we had that case all stinking wrong, all through the trial saying Afghan, Afghan, Afghan when the man was really from Iran, Eduardo got something out of the experience. I expect that Eduardo Americano," said Peggy, "is never going to call anybody a raghead again!"

Edward's recollection is different. "The judge, the D.A., even the public defender," he said, long after completing his sentence, "tried to make this into some kind of hate thing, 'cause that's what they were thinking about. That fight had nothing to do with racism, but everybody was thinking about racism, so I got the extra sentence."

Edward sighed, struggling to draw meaning from the muddle. "I did learn about the Afghan culture, which was a good thing," he concluded finally. "But then I heard the guy was from Persia or something. He wasn't wearing a turban or anything like that, so I'm not sure. I still don't know what country he was from and it don't matter, because I never said he don't belong in this country. I'm Mexican. Why would I be telling anyone that?"

MUSLIM COMMUNITY CENTER, INTERFAITH MEMORIAL SERVICE, San Francisco
First Anniversary of September 11

The Reverend Charles Gibbs (left) was among those praying at the mosque: "The Bay Area's diversity makes
for an extraordinary experiment in human history. It's not a melting pot here, it's an attempt to say be
who you are—but then let's come together and be something more. To pray in a community that was really
alight with that on the September 11 anniversary was inspiring to me. On one level that gathering was
entirely unremarkable—and yet it was world changing, in Gandhi's notion that we must be the change we
wish to see in the world."

BLACK COWBOY PARADE, Oakland

Henry Linzie is the president of the Black Cowboys Association: "I love Bonanza *and all them cowboy pictures, but they never had no black cowboys. All people see on TV is black stable hands shoeing horses.*

"I was born here in Oakland, but my father's from Oklahoma, my mother's from Texas. I knew for a fact that black people were cowboys, and I started riding when I was five years old. But when I wore my cowboy hat and boots around this city, everyone laughed, told me there's no black cowboys.

"We had a hard time convincing the city council to do our first parade in 1974, because they said it wasn't possible for horses to be in Oakland. But we dug up research and showed them that horses went right down Broadway in the 1900s, so we could do it now, it's our history. Finally they had to give it up and we had our parade.

"Everybody wants to know about the black cowboys now, and people don't laugh at us no more. It's a joy to ride in Oakland and let our families, friends, neighbors, and the city know we're not just riding for ourselves, we're riding for history."

Gregory McDowell

MUSICIANS WITH THE BAY AREA BALINESE ORCHESTRA GAMELAN SEKAR JAYA, San Francisco

Scott Barnes, third musician from the left: "My first reaction to the photo is that we all look kind of silly. Dressing up is part of the fun, but it would also be disrespectful not to dress up. There's a fair amount of cultural divergence in the band, but to some extent we're all outsiders. The Balinese musicians are here from Bali, so this isn't their home. The rest of us are coming to the music from somewhere else. So we're all in the same boat—and the outsider becomes the insider. We played in Bali in 2000 and I pondered what the Balinese thought when they saw us. But the response was overwhelming. They really cheered us on."

OVER THIRTY YEARS AGO, THE UNIVERSITY OF CALIFORNIA'S INSTITUTE of Governmental Studies released an incendiary report about the Bay Area's future. Its authors predicted persistent, violent racial clashes within a region almost evenly divided between black and white residents. Despite the fact that the U.S. Immigration Act of 1965 had already abolished longstanding quotas on immigrants according to national origin, thereby opening America's doors to people from all over the world, the prospect of a far more varied and complex Bay Area received no attention.

Yet to be fair, thirty years ago almost nobody could have foreseen the ways in which the Bay Area's reshuffled ethnic mix would change not only the terms of local conflicts, but also our daily habits and preferences—all through the unpredictable power of proximity.

Take, for example, Oakland's Sun Hop Fat #1 Supermarket, located a few blocks south of Lake Merritt on East 12th Street—and its bright and spotless storefront sign advertising:

AMERICAN-MEXICAN-CHINESE-VIETNAMESE-THAILAND-
CAMBODIA-LAOS-FILIPINO-ORIENTAL FOOD

Inside, the market bustles with Saturday shoppers, half of them Asian, the remainder almost evenly divided between Latinos and blacks. In narrow rows of shelving, the foods sort out initially by ethnic preference and then, like the neighborhood outside, the items begin to bleed into one another: the green pepper sauces of Thailand abutting the orange habañeros of Mexico, jars of pickled mud fish and Laotian guava paste sharing shelf space with Albers grits and Hamburger Helper. By the time shoppers reach the checkout counter, the fare has become hopelessly hybrid, the contents of many carts determined less by tradition and habit than crossbred opportunity. Filipino macapuno string is purchased along with frozen jackfruit, Cool Whip, and a six-pack of Dos Equis. A sack of tortillas accompanies a can of roasted peanuts seasoned with cuttlefish powder. In matters of personal taste, consistency seems pointless, if not impossible.

A few blocks away on International Boulevard, known until 1996 as East 14th Street, when the name was changed to coincide with neighborhood realities. Soon the sounds and scents of

India Independence Day, Fremont

amalgamated Southeast Asian Oakland disappear amid the rush of immigrants from Mexico and Central America. By the time you reach Fruitvale Avenue, it's another world.

The first thing you notice is the immense energy of public life. These days, it's the immigrants who are marrying, having kids, and staying married in percentages that surpass the larger society, and this tendency is reflected in the Fruitvale District's bustle. Latino men and women push prams, tote babies on their shoulders, and grasp the hands of their toddlers as crowds swish past to conduct the day's domestic duties. Behind the rows of taquerías, small markets, and a gaudy neon sign advertising the local curandera, a vast open air plaza sprawls, encompassing the BART and bus stations, a score of locally owned stores, the César E. Chávez branch of the Oakland Public Library, Las Bougainvilleas senior center, and nearly fifty new housing units. The plaza is filled with young families, teenagers, and the elderly, and collectively they are reclaiming a neighborhood that for decades proved too dreary, dangerous, and empty for play and leisure. It's here, amid the formerly abandoned commercial strips, public parks, and city squares that family life, long on the fray throughout America, is being mended and renewed.

Yet while the flavor of the Fruitvale is undeniably Latin, and the streets echo with the sounds of Spanish inflected by the regional accents of Mexico and Central America, the district embraces a wider world than first glance suggests. Nearly half the population is foreign-born, and the Fruitvale's residents variously hail from Bosnia, Herzegovina, China, Vietnam, and Cambodia, as well as El Salvador, Guatemala, Mexico, and Honduras. What's unspoken—and perhaps literally unspeakable, given that nearly half of the district's immigrant households cannot effectively communicate in any language other than their own—is the shared quality of hurt that also informs the neighborhood.

The immigrant culture of the Fruitvale, along with much of the Bay Area, is also a refugee culture, framed in bloodshed, death, eviction from longstanding homelands, and evacuation to an unfamiliar country. The keynote of refugee culture is tragedy, its overtone lasting trauma. If the residents of this most densely populated district in the East Bay could convey their experience in a common tongue that communicated beyond their native Spanish, Khmer, Quechua, Bosnian, or Vietnamese, they could tell strikingly similar stories of rivers forded in the dead of night; of the hail of bullets at their backs; of theft, rape, and murder at the hands of bandits on the uncertain road to safety; of the persistent daily difficulty in adapting to their new country. El Mezote, Srebrenicia, Cambodia's Killing Fields, and Tiananmen Square: these place names, synonymous with state-sponsored slaughter, remain both immutable in memory and untranslatable to the larger population. The district's refugees share a common experience of suffering. And yet they remain invisible—even to one another.

Day of the Virgin of Guadalupe, St. Mary's Cathedral, San Francisco

DANIEL DENTON AND ADALBERTO MADRIGAL SAT ON THE FLOOR OF THE HAYWARD MOSQUE, LEGS tucked under them, shoulders almost touching. As their teacher, Imam Zaid Shakir, silently paced the front of the classroom, the two young men bowed their heads and narrowed their eyes, concentrating intensely on the day's Arabic grammar lesson.

A mahogany screen divided the classroom into equal halves, separating men from women. At the front, the imam glanced from side to side to take in a full view of his students. All the women wore head scarves, many covered their faces with veils. Two entirely concealed their bodies under black, featureless burkas. The male students resembled Daniel and Adalberto: serious men in their twenties and thirties assembled in orderly rows on floor pillows, balancing notebooks on their crossed legs. Every man wore a beard, and each covered his head with a white muslin skullcap, turban, or fez.

The imam hummed a sinuous, nasal melody, and the men and women gazed up from their notebooks. "We will sing this song of devotion in each class," announced Imam Zaid, "and soon, God be willing, we will sound like—I shouldn't say it—the Muslim Tabernacle Choir."

Daniel laughed, turned to Adalberto—a fellow Mexican immigrant who had recently converted to Islam—and cried out in Spanish, *"Órale!"* The two men exchanged high-fives, then Adalberto attempted to calm Daniel, whispering, *"Cállate*, hermano." They looked with concern at Imam Zaid. His head was bent forward over his book, but he was smiling. Then the imam's voice rose in song, and Daniel and Adalberto switched from Spanish to Arabic to sing Allah's praise.

Daniel had strayed from Catholicism long before arriving in California. "As a kid in Mexico," he recalled, "I could never figure out that three-in-one thing, the Father, the Son, and the Holy Ghost. When I saw God in my mind, I wasn't seeing Jesus."

The church's seeming indifference to pervasive suffering in Mexico troubled Daniel. "There were beggars on the steps of the cathedral," he said, "with no shoes, torn up pants, greeting you with their hands out. But the church had new stained glass windows and fresh paint on the wall. That never made sense to me."

Daniel gave up on the Catholic church while still living in Mexico. He found Islam after he came to California.

Shaykh Salek bin Siddina, from Mauritania, at the Hayward mosque

Imam Zaid Shakir

On the other side of the room, Daniel's wife, Roxanne, peered through slots in the partition, catching a glimpse of her husband's dark hair spilling out from under his skullcap. Since their first meeting, arranged through Muslim friends, Roxanne had been impressed by Daniel's seriousness. She took note of his devotion and respect for his six siblings and his mother, as befits a good Muslim man. That devotion was now focused on Roxanne, the mother of his two daughters. And it was the couple's dedication to Islam that would soon carry their family from Hayward to the deserts of Sudan.

Daniel and Roxanne had chosen to resettle in Sudan—a country ruled by *sharia*, the laws of Islam. Daniel had selected a village from an Internet search for "Islamic centers of learning." The town proved so small he couldn't find it on a map. "We'll be able to study the Koran in the traditional way," he told Roxanne, "one-on-one with the imam, squatting on the floor, writing with ink made from coal, a twig for our pens—the authentic, uncontaminated way of learning."

The young couple barely discussed the civil war in Sudan—the most longstanding armed conflict in Africa, two million dead, the country incapacitated for decades. It was a war of Muslims against Christians.

When Imam Zaid chanted *Allahu Akbar*—God is Great—Roxanne glanced again at Daniel, then turned toward Mecca and lowered her forehead to the ground in prayer.

AT THE END OF THE TWO-HOUR CLASS, THE STUDENTS FILED TO THE PATIO IN FRONT OF THE MOSQUE. The women set out an urn of tea and platters of dates. But Daniel, Adalberto, and the other Mexicans and Central Americans who had converted to Islam soon after coming to the United States ignored the refreshments and walked to an adjacent dirt field.

"*Assalam alaikoom!*" Daniel tapped his hand over his heart as he greeted Walter Gómez, a Salvadoran immigrant who was blowing on hot coals arrayed in a portable barbecue. "*Alaikoom assalam,*" replied Walter. He cut beef and chicken into strips, then called out in Spanish for Adalberto to bring more tortillas.

Adalberto strolled over in his loose-fitting Moroccan djellaba, bearing fresh tortillas. He had arrived in Hayward from Chicago only a week before, aiming to advance his Islamic studies.

Hayward is a working class town south of Oakland with a large Spanish-speaking population and a recent inflow of Asian and Indian immigrants. Along Mission Boulevard, the city's main drag, taquerías and Peruvian seafood restaurants alternate with halal meat markets and sushi bars. The mosque was cloistered behind divisions of postwar stucco tract homes, its yard bordered by concrete pillars elevating the BART trains. Thousands of commuters sped by each day over tracks skirting the mosque, never dreaming it was there.

Daniel, Adalberto, and Walter tucked back the loose sleeves of their djellabas to avoid grease spatter from the barbecue, then tossed tortillas, chicken, and beef on the grill for a traditional Mexican *asada*. As they prepared taquitos for two dozen hungry Muslims, they switched from English and Arabic to their native Spanish. They joked with Adalberto about his fiancée, whom he had first set eyes on only days before, matchmaking being one of the benefits of community life. They bantered in Spanglish about their favorite Arabic foods: "*Tan picante*, man, so spicy *que puede* knock you out!" They talked about their Muslim *hermanos y hermanas* in their expanding Islamic *familia*, which included Yemeni men who had married *mujeres de México*. "The Yemenis are attracted to *las mujeres Mexicanas* more than to white women," said Daniel, "because Mexican women are more modest and proper."

Finally, speaking of the hardships and uncertainties Daniel and his family would face in their imminent move to the Sudan, Adalberto's Spanish failed him. "*Insha'Allah,*" he said solemnly in Arabic. God be willing.

While grilling the last batch of *pollo asado*, Daniel and Adalberto drifted into reminiscences about their childhoods in Mexico, insisting that their conversions to Islam had been a homecoming for them. Islam evoked the spirit of a Mexico of families bound together by religion. A Mexico of *La Virgen* and *El Padre*, of strong, loving mothers and stern fathers. A Mexico of tradition, rules, and morals, where religious ritual and faith permeated every aspect of life. But although they would not admit it, they were speaking of a Mexico not of their memories, but their dreams—an idealization of family and tradition largely unfulfilled for them in Mexico, yet sorely missed in the United States.

Adalberto spoke of his family's weekly *asadas*—his father, mother, eleven sisters, two brothers, cousins, aunts, and uncles gathered about a barbecue pit at their Jalisco home. "We fought and argued, too," he acknowledged, "but we were there with the whole family. That was the important part."

At seventeen, Adalberto joined his sister in Chicago, and immediately descended into a life of drugs, gangs, and promiscuity. When Spanish-speaking Anglo Mormons befriended him, he proved ripe for conversion. For two years, he threw himself into the life of the Church of Jesus Christ of Latter-day Saints.

Then he discovered Islam. In a Chicago neighborhood filled with Palestinian and Jordanian immigrants, an imam gave Adalberto a Spanish translation of the Koran. He devoured the book in a week. Then the Jordanians invited him to eat in their homes and discuss the teachings of Muhammad.

Adalberto was struck by the courtesy of his new Muslim friends, their offerings of food, their kindness toward him, a stranger. "Muslims are family oriented, very similar to Mexicans," he recalled later. "Their family gatherings were like my family gatherings. The Muslims felt very familiar, like I knew them for a long, long time." His conversion to Islam made life in the United States less stressful and lonely, more warm and intimate.

"Here in the U.S. you don't even say hello to your neighbor," he said. "But the Muslims are different. They see me on the street and say, *'Assalam alaikoom,'* and I say, *'Alaikoom assalam.'* It's like *buenos días.* It's like Mexico."

WHEN DANIEL WAS A STUDENT AT SAN JOAQUIN DELTA COLLEGE, IN THE CENTRAL VALLEY, HIS HISTORY professor assigned the class an essay: "Who was the most important individual in shaping the world?" Daniel chose Alexander the Great; the Muslims in the class selected Muhammad, the prophet of Islam.

"I looked at Islam with more interest," recalled Daniel. "Here's this great leader. I gotta check him out."

During Ramadan, the holy month during which Muslims fast from dawn to dusk, Daniel persuaded his Mexican friends to support their Islamic cohorts by joining their fast. By the second day, all of Daniel's Latino friends were devouring midday hamburgers. But Daniel held the fast. "It humbled me," he said. "I went through such dramatic changes, they amazed me."

Daniel besieged his Muslim friends with scores of questions about their culture. The Islamic emphasis on charity, hospitality, and family impressed him deeply.

He also discovered—and embraced—the Islamic prohibition against alcohol.

Heavy drinking had long been a tradition in Daniel's family. "My grandfather had an alcohol problem and he committed suicide," he said. "My uncle used to send me to get him rubbing alcohol, he was that desperate to drink. And when I lived with my mom in Tijuana, I'd be out partying every night."

Soon after his Ramadan fast, Daniel quit drinking. His family viewed his sobriety with suspicion. "I was living with my aunt," he said. "She got worried because I wasn't eating and I started losing weight. My beard was kind of long and I was reading books about Islam. So my aunt called my mom and said I was doing drugs and had become a terrorist."

Daniel finished the semester, then went to see his mother. "I told her about Islam," he said, "and she just stayed quiet. But my sisters said that after I left, my mom cried all night. I told them I'd been kneeling and putting my face in the dirt to pray to God, so I'm not thinking about booze or partying anymore."

Soon Daniel was unfurling his prayer rug five times a day. But when a Muslim friend invited him to pray at the local mosque, he hesitated. "I didn't think I had the right to pray at a mosque," he said, "because I wasn't really a Muslim."

Finally, he accompanied his friend into a large apartment, the floors covered by rugs, the rooms painted white but otherwise unadorned. There were no chairs, pews, paintings, or statues. The makeshift mosque bore little resemblance to the churches where Daniel had worshipped as a child.

An imam conducted the service in Arabic. "I just sat there, observing," said Daniel, "soaking it in. There were black people, white people, a lot of Arabs. No Mexicans."

By the end of the evening, Daniel was sitting on the floor next to an elderly Muslim man. "He was telling me all about the beliefs of Islam," said Daniel. "And I was saying, yes, yes, I believe in that."

"There is one God."

"Yes, yes."

"The Prophet Muhammad, peace be upon him, was God's final messenger. Jesus, peace be upon him, was also a prophet. But he is not God."

"Yes."

"God, who we call Allah, knows what is in our hearts."

"Yes."

"Muslims must seek knowledge, since this is the best way to know Allah."

"Yes."

"The word Islam means peace, and submission to God."

"Yes."

On the spot, the man invited Daniel to become a Muslim.

"My family flashed before my eyes," remembered Daniel, "and I thought, 'They're going to disown me! My mom's going to be heartbroken.' But I was stuck, because I believed in what that man was telling me. And on the day of judgment it's going to be just me and God. I held the old man's hand and he said, 'Repeat after me. *La ilaha ila Allah; Muhammadur-rasul Allah.*'"

Daniel asked the man to say it again in English.

"There is no God apart from God, and Muhammad is God's messenger."

"I repeated the words," recalled Daniel, "and the man said, 'That's it. You're a Muslim.'"

Adalberto prepares carne asada and tortillas

FOR DANIEL AND ADALBERTO, ISLAM PROVIDED CLEAR MORAL GROUND IN WHICH TO SPREAD THEIR roots—precisely at a time when their young lives had seemed most out of control. Yet they discarded the notion that they'd been merely seeking a return to traditions, or fleeing alcohol or their isolation as immigrants.

Daniel and Adalberto believed their embrace of Islam represented a historical validation of their true Spanish heritage. The Islamic Moors, they reasoned, had conquered Spain in the eighth century and maintained a presence until their final rout by the Christians in 1492—the same year that Columbus set out on a journey that initiated the Christian conquest of the New World. Daniel and Adalberto's conversion from Mexican to Muhammadan, they said, was a throwing off of two conquests—a journey back to their Moorish roots in Spain.

For Daniel, the link of Moorish to Mexican culture confirmed the rightness of his conversion, and strengthened his resolve to move his family to Sudan.

DANIEL AND ROXANNE PUSHED PITCHFORKS INTO THE EARTH OF THE VEGETABLE GARDEN BEHIND THE Hayward mosque. As the sun reached its zenith, the chant of the call to prayer interrupted their work. Allahu Akbar. The voice of the muezzin surged from the loudspeaker, each repetition more drawn out, radiating from the mosque as if carried on a desert wind.

They dropped their pitchforks to the earth and entered the ritual washing rooms to prepare for the noon prayer. Adalberto joined Daniel on the men's side. The two squatted below a water tap protruding from a white tiled wall to perform the *wuduu*, the traditional ablution that precedes Islamic prayer.

Adalberto poured water from his left hand to his right and washed up to his wrist three times. "My father washed in this exact way," he told Daniel. "My uncles did, too. And all of us kids, we never asked why, we just did it."

The two men brought their hands to their mouths and sniffed water into their nostrils, then blew it out, three times.

"Where'd your father learn it?" asked Daniel.

Adalberto's great-great-grandfather, he told Daniel, had come to Mexico from the south of Spain, Andalusia, the land of the Moors. His family, generation after generation of Mexican Catholics, had continued performing the ritual Islamic washing.

A WEEK LATER, DANIEL AND ROXANNE STOOD ON THE SIDEWALK IN FRONT OF THEIR SINGLE-STORY GRAY stucco home, airplane tickets and passports in hand. They chatted calmly with friends about their family's upcoming flight—San Francisco to Frankfurt to Bahrain, then finally Khartoum, Sudan.

The U.S. State Department had announced that week the barest glimmer of hope for peace in Sudan—a glimmer that would soon be extinguished.

Daniel stood in front of his house alongside fifteen three-foot-square sealed cardboard boxes, struggling to reach Sudan on his cell phone. He listened to the silence, then slipped the phone back into his pocket and smiled sheepishly. "It's futile," said Daniel, and he went back to writing his address on the air-freight cartons.

In preparation for their new life in Sudan, Daniel had packed some modern, Western conveniences: a fax machine; books for his daughters (along with packages of macaroni and cheese); pamphlets on canning fruits and vegetables, purifying water, and building super-adobe heat-resistant houses in the desert.

As a young American father about to deliver his family into the uncertainties of Muslim life in Sudan, Daniel had chosen carefully among tools, materials, and mementos that might unite his Mexican heritage with his new Islamic life, and an unpredictable future.

Shaykh Salek bin Siddina, from Mauritania, at the noon prayer with (from right) Adalberto and Daniel

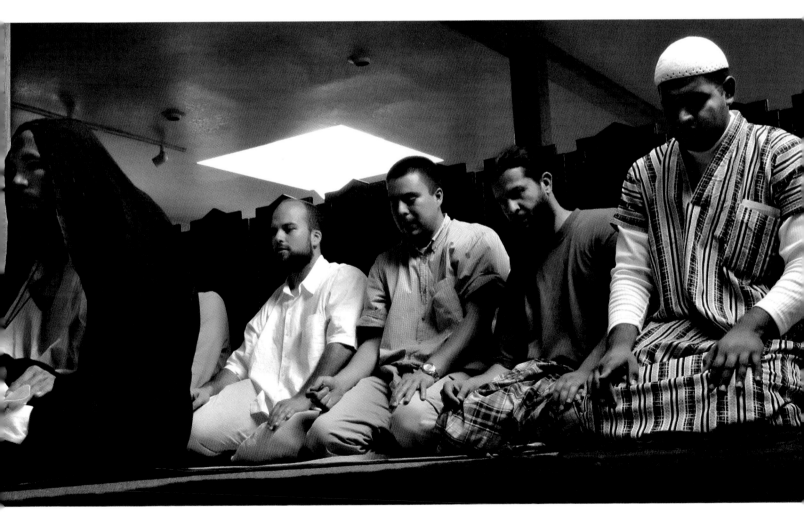

Noura Erakat is a founding member of Students for Justice in Palestine: "That Palestinian man is thinking, 'I'm going to die in this country, I'll never go home to Palestine.' The injustice by the Israelis runs so deep he feels like he's being persecuted by Nazis. I want to tell him, 'Uncle, Ame, have hope, and put down the flag with the swastika. If you have to carry a flag, carry the Palestinian flag. It represents an identity, a home, and a future.'

"That Jewish guy with the flag probably lived through the Holocaust and he can't be reasonable about the Palestinian situation. For him, it's a completely emotional response. And he's given money to the Israeli government for what in fact is aggression against Palestinians. I wouldn't talk to him."

Rabbi Yehudah Ferris is the director of Chabad of Berkeley: "The man with the Israeli flag is patriotic, a Zionist with a defiantly serene look, a proper guy. I'd love to have lunch with him.

"The face of the guy with the Nazi flag is etched with tzuris, trouble and misfortune. He's saying Israel is a racist, oppressive Nazi regime, with targeted assassinations and helicopter gunships. I feel bad for him, because he's making a moral equivalent between Israelis and Nazis that doesn't exist. As long as Palestinians call for the destruction of the state of Israel, they can't be trusted.

"Thank God I was born after World War II, so the swastika doesn't rip at my gut like for my parents and grandparents. I think what he's doing with the swastika is intolerable. They would punch him in the nose."

BERKELEY HIGH SCHOOL GRADUATION, Berkeley

Berkeley High School's Japanese American students who were taken to internment camps at the start of World War II were made honorary graduates in 2004.

Margaret Kusaba, seventy-nine, was removed from Berkeley High School when she was seventeen and sent to the Topaz internment camp in Utah: "My parents were Americans and I was born here, so it didn't dawn on me they'd take us. It was so windy and dusty at Topaz we had to cover our faces. Then when we came back to Berkeley after the war, the neighborhood was mostly blacks and they were not welcoming. I never felt at ease.

"After 9/11 there was talk about rounding up Islamic people. It brought back memories. But this graduation showed that people do care for us—they brought a car to pick me up and the students gave a standing ovation—it brought tears. That girl behind me is wearing African colors. I think it's a good change, their being able to express themselves, be proud of who they are."

KWANZAA, Oakland
Deborah Jackson

*Deborah Jackson is the director of the Luxor Academy, a black private school in Oakland: "Kwanzaa is
not an African holiday—it is an African American holiday, to rebuild the spirit of who we are as a people.
People do not understand our culture—that we are family oriented and grounded, not about gangs and
violence. The Bay Area has done well with diversity, but we have a long way to go because African American
people are still at the bottom. So when you talk about diversity and opportunities, I am asking are we really
looking at equality? Or are we playing at it, calling it diversity? What's really happening here?"*

THAI NEW YEAR, Fremont
Phramaha Singho Punnamedho receives New Year food offerings

Phra Videsdhan Makavi is the head monk at Wat Buddhanusorn, a Thai temple in Fremont: "Thai Buddhist monks are not allowed to make a living, so people must feed us. In Thailand, we walk the streets with alms bowl. In Fremont is different. Every day Thai American people bring us good food from Thai restaurants, more than we need. For Thai monk, begging is not a bad thing. But American people don't like begging—they see us like homeless people and feel bad. We are not homeless people. We are Thai monks."

ALONE TOGETHER AT WORK AND SCHOOL

ONE FORCE HAS CONSISTENTLY DRAWN PEOPLE TO THE SAN FRANCISCO Bay Area: the promise of work.

In 1848, the year before the gold rush, San Francisco barely existed; the city's non-native population was estimated at a scant six hundred souls. Four years later, some forty thousand residents had materialized, forming an instant city of fortune seekers. Laborers and tradesmen fleeing the potato famine in Ireland and the revolutions of central Europe mixed with thousands of would-be miners rushing in from Australia, Peru, Hawai'i, China, and France. By 1880, immigrants or first-generation Americans constituted 60 percent of the population. North Beach began as a Chilean neighborhood. A half-dozen "Chinatowns" sprang up on both sides of the bay. Then, as now, many of the jobs that the new arrivals fought for, blundered into, or created for themselves were hewn along ethnic lines.

San Francisco's large immigrant Irish neighborhoods south of Market Street served as spawning grounds for several generations of police and firefighters. Crews manning the lumber schooners that dotted the bay hailed from Sweden, Denmark, and Norway, thus earning the sobriquet "Scandinavian navy." In Hayward and San Leandro, the Portuguese labored seasonally in the orchards and then filed into the canneries. Greeks operated small cafés near the West Oakland train terminal, Slavs vied with Sicilians for dominion over the fishing industry, and Italians from all parts of the boot harvested grapes in Livermore's vineyards, raised and sold artichokes and cabbages along the San Mateo coast, and organized companies to haul trash from the urban core out to vast mounds of refuse on the shorelines.

Today we can observe similar patterns of specialization born of kinship and necessity. When you catch a cab home from the San Francisco International Airport, you may be transported by a Christian Assyrian from Iraq operating under the shield of the Luxor Cab Company. Should you drop by before work at your local doughnut shop, you're likely to be served by Cambodian immigrants, who have been operating franchises since the 1980s. The men assembled in road gangs to patch potholes and repave the streets—the precise origin of their Spanish accent unrecognized by all but their fellow countrymen—are probably Peruvian. Each day, the women from Mexico, Brazil, Guatemala, and the Philippines who care for upper middle class children of all races can be found pushing five-hundred-dollar

Immigrants from Oaxaca, Mexico, just arrived in San Francisco

Bertini double 4X4 prams along Lakeshore Avenue in Oakland and in San Francisco's Marina District—or cleaning houses practically anywhere in the Bay Area, their chief qualification being a willingness to dispatch one of the many jobs that most other Americans no longer want to do. Throughout the week, lines of day laborers assemble at sunrise on the corner of Fruitvale Avenue and International Boulevard, along César Chávez Street in the Outer Mission, at busy intersections in downtown San Rafael and suburban Newark—all dependable places to find a Latino, Chinese, or Southeast Asian immigrant to dig a hole, climb a roof, or build a second-story addition to a suburban home. The presence and numbers of these people, along with their avidity for hard work, underscore the fact that the Bay Area, along with the rest of the nation, is more dependent on immigrant labor than at any time in the past one hundred years.

The last era in which the Bay Area witnessed such an infusion of willing brawn was during World War II—a "Second Gold Rush" that not only sparked new industries within a revitalized economy, but also drastically sifted the regional mix of ethnicity and culture. At the height of war production, the Alameda Naval Air Station and Mare Island in Vallejo employed more than 40,000 workers with long-sought Federal regulations opening up many jobs to African Americans for the first time. The Kaiser shipyards in Richmond hired more than 100,000 people, including laborers recruited from Nicaragua and El Salvador who reseeded the Latin base of Oakland's Fruitvale District, while many Chinese laborers gained entry into high-wage union jobs.

Today virtually all the era's military bases and private defense contractors have closed up shop—with much of the area's heavy industry following suit. In Hayward, Hunt's cannery once ran around-the-clock shifts at twin factories, filling the air with the sickly-sweet scent of stewed tomatoes for four months out of the year. In Fremont, General Motors operated the largest automobile assembly plant in California. Sweat and muscle now seldom ensure the economic security they provided in the recent past. With pressure from technological change, global competition, and declining unionization, recent immigrants—and even more, their children—must achieve far higher levels of education to secure jobs that will advance their family income.

Yet state-wide, 72 percent of the adults who have failed to complete high school are immigrants—and more worrisome, a substantial share of their children appear to be opting out of the educational opportunities never afforded their parents. For Latinos, graduation rates fall well below 60 percent. The direst news involves the recent arrivals from Mexico, by far the largest immigrant group in the Bay Area, who acquire less education than other groups and as a direct result, straggle behind in terms of lifetime earnings. Indeed, as one recent study of income and education by the Public Policy Institute of California concludes: "Intergenerational progress for Mexican Americans appears to stall after the second generation, with only modest improvement in educational attainment and no wage growth observed between the second and third generations."

For the poor, uneducated, and recently arrived, education remains essential. And yet the public schools routinely falter at their traditional role of integrating newcomers into the larger society.

"I remember the first dance I supervised," recalled Rob Jones, a young African American teacher at Helms Middle School in Richmond. "I was looking for one of my students, a Laotian boy named Chao. And a black kid told me: 'Oh, he's over in the Asian corner.' I couldn't believe my eyes. My students had all walked out of class together—black, Asian, Latino. But as soon as they entered the gym, the Asian kids formed a circle in one corner with all the boys break-dancing in the center. The black kids grouped near the speakers, dancing hip-hop style. The Latinos bunched up at the edge of the black kids. And the school's handful of white kids and weird kids were milling around the periphery by the cotton candy booth. Everybody's listening to Bow Wow, Ying Yang Twins, or Ludacris—all black hip-hop artists—but there's not one couple from different ethnic groups dancing together."

"In class, it's different," added Sam Franklin, a 25-year-old white teacher at Elmhurst Middle School in East Oakland, and Rob's closest friend. "I've never had an issue of one kid refusing to work with another because of his ethnicity. It's more like, 'I'm not working with this kid 'cause…*he sucks*.' Kids segregate along levels of coolness as well as race. At lunch, the confident, socially competent Asian, black, and Latino kids sit with the cool kids of their own race. But if you're not in with the main crew, if you're an awkward nerd, you're likely to be sitting with nerds from all the other ethnic groups. The nerd table is the most mixed table."

And where are the white kids in the public schools of Richmond and Oakland?

"In both of our schools," said Rob, "if there's a white kid, he's guaranteed to be the most uncomfortable, odd, weird-situation kid ever. To be white and still living in this neighborhood where all the other whites managed to get out, you got to figure something's messed up in that family system…"

"Just the same," said Sam, "all the other kids certainly have an image of white people. It just doesn't come from meeting any. It's like a white rich kid growing up in the suburbs, but figuring what he's seen on hip-hop videos is the total sum of black people's lives. That's the way black kids in East Oakland think about white people. They know all about them—from what they've seen on TV."

Laotian American (Mien) athletes at predominantly black Oakland High School

NEWLY MIEN UNDER THE AMERICAN SUN

A Traditional Mien Dance

NINETEEN-YEAR-OLD LINDA NAI SAEVANG STARED INTO THE MIRROR AS SHE WRAPPED THE CLOTH OF HER her vivid indigo turban once, twice, then over and over around her head. She sighed in frustration at the turban's awkward tilt, a perceptible drift from the distinctive symmetry of traditional Mien headgear.

Another pair of hands fell reassuringly on her shoulders, then unwrapped the twenty-foot length of embroidered cloth. In the Mien language, Linda's mother urged calm. They'd been at it for forty-five minutes. Together, they wound the cloth again until it was angled just so, framing Linda's forehead in an overlapping crisscross of folds in the style her mother had worn when she lived in Laos.

But Linda, born in a Thai refugee camp after her family fled Laos, transported to the United States at age two, had never lived the daily life of the Laotian mountain tribe. This was only her fifth attempt at the Mien turban.

"When I was your age," said Linda's mom, "we wrapped our heads and decorated our clothes with silver jewelry every morning. I needed only a few minutes to get my turban on right."

Linda closed her eyes, trying to call up the image. To her, Laos was a figment of folk tales, the ancestral homeland, unimaginable. Even less plausible were her parents' tales of the American CIA trekking into the mountains of Laos during the height of the Vietnam War to enlist the aid of the Mien tribes to fight the communists. When the Americans lost the war, those Mien who had worked with the CIA fled to Thailand. Then they were evacuated to the United States.

America imposed distinct and contradictory obligations on Linda's generation. *Join the dominant culture. Maintain your own culture. Don't stick out. Distinguish yourself. Stay faithful to the Mien. Prove you are an American. Show this country who you are.* Linda glanced about the room at fourteen young Mien American men and women aided by their mothers and grandmothers in an attempt at looking Mien. They were students at the University of California, Davis, dressing for their debut performance as the Mien Dance Troupe at the campus's annual Asian-Pacific Culture Night.

Linda's friend Chan Saechao sidled over, the silver bells on her blouse pinging as she turned and asked Linda why she was taking so long getting dressed. Linda crinkled her forehead in a plea for forbearance. Her eyes shifted in the direction of her mother, indicating where the problem lay.

"She's tripping 'cause it's not exactly right," said Linda.

Kao Cheng Saephanh

"It's not straight yet!" insisted her mother in Mien, shaking her head for Chan to leave them be. In each corner of the suburban tract home, young Mien straightened silver necklaces under bulging red collars while their mothers tightened thick sashes about their waists. One student asserted she would wear the turban when she married.

But how did she know she would marry a Mien? These were modern, second-generation Mien Americans studying economics, finance, and marketing. Their friends were Chinese, Filipino, Latino, Ethiopian, European, Canadian. One of the Mien students studied Spanish at the university. "You should speak it," she reasoned, "if you live in California." They were realists. How Mien would they be after graduate school and the pursuit of split-level tract homes like the one they were now using to dress for their dance?

But on this day, the Mien students were intent on drawing fragments of their past into the present. They were shaping a response to that particular demand of America—*show us who you are*—by looking backwards, for the moment, to Laos.

Her turban finally in place, Linda tramped barefoot across the plush carpet and announced to her friends that she was ready. The mothers gathered around their children for a final inspection. All agreed that their children appeared dignified, correct, presentable.

The families, fathers now joining in as well, streamed out the front door, pausing to pick their shoes out from the dozens on the doorstep. They piled into cars and drove to the UC Davis campus, where, in a cavernous, packed auditorium, the young Mien would perform a traditional dance.

None of the Mien students seemed at all bothered by the fact that, in Laos, performances of Mien music and dance do not exist.

IN THE BASEMENT REHEARSAL SECTION OF THE AUDITORIUM, TWENTY MEMBERS OF A FILIPINO DANCE troupe slipped into silk costumes and waved ceremonial swords. Chinese acrobats erupted into somersaults. Nostalgic Persuasion, a Korean American rap group, boomed rhymes into microphones at deafening decibels. A troupe of buff young Hawai'ian men flexed their biceps and thrust pointed spears into the air.

Linda Saevang and
Koy Pou Saelee

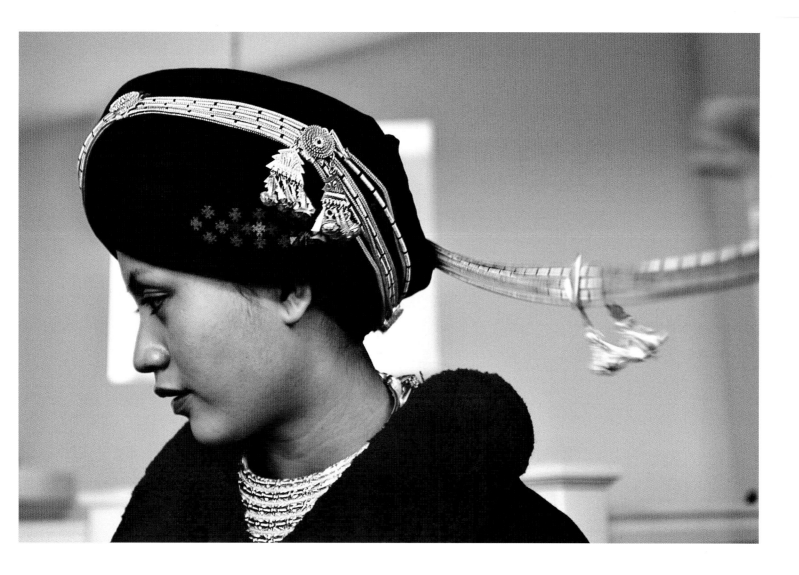

Chan Saechao

Rehearsing for the dance

Every corner of the auditorium basement was filled with frantic rehearsal—the fine-tuning of complex choreographies that would soon launch Asian-Pacific Culture Night.

When the Mien dance troupe arrived, everybody fell back—the Chinese, Japanese, Hawai'ians, Filipinos, Tongans, Samoans, Koreans, Bhutanese. None of the students, it was safe to say, had ever seen a sight quite like the Mien.

The women shimmered magnificently—silver bells, stars, and dewdrop moons fanning over their coats. The men passed by in sleek black tunics and bright red head wraps. All the Mien held their heads high, necks rigid, balancing their turbans as if they were crowns.

A Korean student asked Linda how long it took for her to dress. "Over an hour," she replied. "And you?"

"Five minutes," he said, and returned to his own dance group.

A buzz of chatter floated through the room. Who were these Mien?

Hill people. Ancient. From Southeast Asia somewhere. Something about the Vietnam War. How did they get here?

To the third-generation Chinese acrobat, the second-generation Filipino swordsman, or the Hawai'ian body builder who visited his grandparents in their Big Island beachfront condo—well, the Mien had to be respected. Old World. The Real Thing. A preliterate culture so recently arrived on American shores that they remained mysteriously, authentically Mien.

Whatever that might mean.

Even the event's organizers had seemed puzzled by the Mien. Months before, when Linda proposed that the Mien perform, one of the student coordinators asked, "Oh, are the Mien Chinese?" "No," replied Linda, "we're Mien. If we were Chinese we'd say so."

Upstairs, two thousand students packed the auditorium. Right on time, the show began. The Filipino dance company amassed on stage and flashed their swords. When they built a pyramid with their silk-clothed bodies, the crowd hooted, jumped to their feet, and applauded insanely. Then the Korean American rap duo strutted across the stage and popped a staccato rhythm of percussive P's into their microphones. The crowd's enthusiasm exceeded its previous summit and the din swelled, leaking out the sealed auditorium doors and into the still air of the warm spring campus evening.

Then it was time for the Mien.

The moment they arrived on stage, the assembly fell silent, as if a volume switch had been dialed quickly down to zero. Fourteen young Mien men and women formed a double line, facing the hushed audience.

The enormous theater speakers poured out the recorded drone of a vocalist's high-pitched falsetto, the language unidentifiable. The dancers strolled across the stage, their wrists flicking, their fingers drawn and then spread, splayed and recoiled, beckoning and then withdrawing. A supple step forward was followed by another to the side, men and women nearly brushing shoulders. Finally, lined up once again, hands peaked like steeples, they bowed gracefully amid the final quiver of plucked strings and the fading whisper of song. The audience remained silent. Mesmerized. Or perhaps bewildered. Then their hands drew into polite applause.

Moments later, the Mien Dance Troupe reassembled in the basement. Each member appeared exhausted from the performance, from the weight of months of rehearsals, from the uncertainty about how their debut had been regarded.

Linda and her fellow dancers could now shrug off the tension borne of the responsibility of presenting Mien culture to the world—and the understanding that to a very large degree, they had made it all up.

"Our parents were really surprised when they watched," said Linda, "because they had never seen that kind of dance before."

Formal dance and music performances are not part of the Mien tradition; they practice both arts only in religious rituals and intimate community ceremonies. The Mien students had learned the dance

The Mien Dance Troupe

steps during their years in the Thai refugee camps, not in Laos. The high, whining music was a six-year-old Thai pop tune, recorded in the United States and sung in Mien. "It has really silly lyrics," admitted Linda, "about guys breaking up with girls."

The Mien dance presentation was a peculiar, unrepeatable event. The young Mien Americans had been children of flight, born in Thai refugee camps, raised in America. Their perspective on Mien culture was unique. They could look—they were compelled to look—toward both past and future, recognizing that their identity had been forged from unequal, unstable measures of several disparate cultures. The invitation to make a public presentation of Mien culture had reflected an American imperative, American assumptions. In responding, the Mien students had invented a tradition—newly Mien under the American sun.

Naked Mien Girls

IT COULD HAVE BEEN THE MEKONG—SOUTHEAST ASIA'S MEANDERING RIVER WHERE REFUGEE BOATS drifted from Laos to the Thai refugee camps. It could have been the Mekong—had the Mien teenagers remembered the Mekong at all while they gathered along the shore of California's Sacramento River.

Mey Saelee crawled out of the water at the river's edge, her hands groping at tree roots protruding from the muddy bank. Gripping one root firmly, she pulled herself onto the shore of the Sacramento River. Mey stood soaking wet, struggling to regain her balance as she called out to her younger sister, Cheng, who had scampered to land just before her. Cheng fastened a Mien necklace about Mey's neck and shoulders, and the silver mesh sparkled in the sunlight. Cheng helped Mey adjust her clothes, pulling lightly at the fabric until all was perfectly set. Mey glanced at her sister for a final nod of approval, then struck her pose.

"Can I see some more breast?" shouted Keith Selle, adjusting his camera's focus while his assistant tilted an oval light reflector to concentrate the sun's glow on Mey's necklace and chest. "Just a little, but no nipple."

Cheng giggled. Then she stretched Mey's clinging wet t-shirt to better expose her breasts under the chest-high logo: *Mien Angels.*

Keith squeezed down on the shutter, then lowered his camera, looking around to plan his next shot. He still hadn't captured the best image of Mey to print as Miss June for the Mien Girls Calendar.

Now twenty-eight, Keith had arrived in California from the Thai refugee camps when he was ten. At twenty-two, he had apprenticed with photographers at *Penthouse* magazine in Los Angeles. Now he called out instructions and Mey unzipped her denim shorts to reveal a sky-blue thong. Her pose projected a perfect blend of blithe innocence and carnality. Keith moved in for a tighter shot.

"I told myself I should do something for my community, so that people in this country will know who the Mien are," he told Mey as his assistants packed up the photo gear to move downriver for the final shots of the day. "They'll see the Mien Girls Calendar and say, 'Wow, the Mien are such a small community, but they did something so important.'"

Further down the river, beside drooping willows, the photo team regrouped. In the soft, shaded light under the trees, Cheng again secured a necklace on her sister.

"Mom says that in Laos, Mien women wore silver all over their clothes," Mey told her younger sister. "It was, you know, status."

Keith hovered about Mey with his camera. "Eyes wider now," he cajoled, "show your tongue, tease me with it." A sparkle of sunlight reflected off the silver stud that pierced Mey's tongue. Keith glanced west, where the sun floated just over the hills along the river. The moment of perfect light had arrived. He had meticulously planned every aspect of the next photograph, destined to grace the back cover of the coming year's calendar. He had even borrowed an elaborate necklace from his mother. Now he checked the angle of the sun, consulted his light meter, set up the reflectors, and called for the girls to join him.

The previous year's calendar, Keith explained, had featured a beautiful Mien woman posed entirely naked except for an unwound Mien turban snaking around her breasts, hips, and thighs, finally flowing into a puddle on the floor. One long leg extended forward, as if she were about to step out from the folds of the turban and into the New World. In the background hung a wall-size American flag.

"I got a lot of feedback about that," admitted Keith. "They said I was destroying Mien culture."

He stepped back, checking the light and composition for the last time. Satisfied, Keith raised the camera to his eye and slowly circled Mey, clicking the shutter again and again. Mey shivered. The wind had picked up. The shoot concluded.

As Keith packed up his gear, Mey called Cheng to her side. She lowered her shorts to just above her buttocks, revealing a new tattoo.

"They're tiger lily pads," explained Mey, "like what the Mien here plant in the summer to remind them of Laos. My friends were saying, 'Why get a tattoo of a plant?' So I'm, like, 'You don't get it. It's a Mien thing.'"

Cheng echoed agreement by lifting her own Mien Angels t-shirt to reveal a tiny silver star in her pierced belly button. "It's like Mom's Mien jewelry," said Cheng. "But mine's got purple stones, too, so it's different."

Cheng turned toward her older sister. "What are you going to say to Mom and Dad about the pictures in the calendar?" she asked.

Mey shook river water from her streaked-blonde hair.

"I'll tell them," she said, "that we're not in Laos anymore."

Mien Angel along the Sacramento River

TIANANMEN SQUARE MASSACRE ANNIVERSARY, CHINATOWN, San Francisco

During the 1989 Tiananmen Square democracy uprising in China, some twenty-six hundred protestors were killed by the Chinese government. Li Lu, a leader of the uprising, was one of the last students to flee before the massacre. Chinese authorities pursued him in an intensive manhunt, but he escaped and now lives in the United States.

Li Lu: "The woman is looking at pictures from that tragic moment when the army opened fire on unarmed people. I cry even now when I see those pictures. It's a deep wound, and it's always there. The Chinese in San Francisco who commemorate Tiananmen's anniversary represent hundreds of millions of Chinese in China who would like to memorialize Tiananmen but can't do it."

MAYA SUNRISE CEREMONY,
Dolores Park, San Francisco
Pascual Yaxón

*Pascual Yaxón was flown to the United States
from Guatemala by San Francisco Mayans
to guide them through the Mayan new year
ceremony: "America doesn't look like America.
All I see are Asians, Latinos, and black people.
Where are the Americans? I asked the Mayans,
and they said you don't see Americans on the
streets, or on buses or trains. The Americans
stay in their houses and their cars. In Guatemala the Mayans are a hidden people. Invisible. But here the Mayans seem more visible
than the Americans."*

NATIONAL ORIGINS: PRIDE, CONFUSION, AND LOSS

WELCOME TO SAI GON NHO—LITTLE SAIGON

So reads the red and yellow banner flying from the streetlamp in San Francisco's Tenderloin District—the city's official designation for the two-block portion of Larkin Street between Eddy and O'Farrell. Out of twenty-eight thousand residents inhabiting the neighborhood's twenty square blocks, Vietnamese account for slightly more than one-tenth of the population. Yet the engine of commerce, some two hundred and fifty businesses covering half of a square mile, remains distinctly in their hands.

Beyond these boundaries, however, confusions easily arise.

When the San Francisco Board of Supervisors voted in 2003 to recognize what supporters called "the sacred Vietnamese Yellow Flag" as the symbol of the city's Vietnamese community, then-Mayor Willie Brown quickly stepped in to veto the resolution. Unbeknownst to the supervisors, the yellow flag was also the symbol of South Vietnam, a country that ceased to exist once it was defeated in 1975 by the North. Citing the "cutting edge" economic relationship between the Socialist Republic of Vietnam and San Francisco, including a sister city relationship established in 1995 with Ho Chi Minh City, the Mayor ended an affair that seemed only to emphasize how little most San Franciscans outside of Sai Gon Nho understood about the thriving community in their midst. "I did not know that this was the exact flag of South Vietnam," admitted Supervisor Fiona Ma, the resolution's sponsor. "That was my bad."

The point, of course, is not the fallibility of public officials, but rather the impossibility of any one person maintaining an intimate acquaintance with the ambitions, conflicts, codes, achievements, and delusions of every community and ethnic enclave within a vast metropolitan mix.

Across the bay in Oakland, Koreatown has sprung up over the past half-dozen years along Telegraph Avenue—despite the absence of Korean residents in the neighborhood. On Saturday afternoons, many of the Bay Area's sixty-four thousand native-born Koreans converge along the twenty-block strip to shop, negotiating with walkie-talkie-wielding parking monitors who direct long lines of cars creeping toward Koreana Plaza, a vast market featuring Korean foods with a Korean video outlet tucked into the corner. The neighborhood still recalls the last vestiges of Oakland's old Scandinavian settlers—from the

A former South Vietnamese soldier during Tet, Vietnamese New Year, Oakland

former Jenny Lind Theatre on the corner of West Grand Avenue (now home to the Minh Yeuh Jin Shyh Buddhist Association of Northern California) to the Nordic House delicatessen selling Danish pastries and Norwegian lutefisk a few blocks away. Yet the signs and iconography of the Telegraph Avenue strip all point to cultural change—occasionally finessing the point with subtle alteration. Kim's Backyard, a local bar first opened by white proprietors, then for decades serving a black clientele—and lit always by an art deco neon sign describing a martini glass with a phosphorescent olive—has added a bottom line of Korean script welcoming the bar's newest customers. And a poster at the front door introduces the current proprietor, the latest Kim, whose face is Korean.

Cities within cities: one runs over, shoves away, or devours another from the inside. Displacement is the pattern of urban life, and whether the resultant changes are regarded as decline, improvements, gentrification, colonization, or the inevitable shift of people and populations, winners and losers always emerge, and the borderlines bristle with ragged edges.

Today some fifteen thousand Afghans inhabit the tract homes of Fremont, Union City, Newark, Hayward, and San Leandro, and many of them frequent Fremont's Little Kabul—an array of shops and stores along Fremont Boulevard at Thornton Avenue. Little Kabul offers what most of the Bay Area cannot: the Pamir Food Mart's selection of flat bread, spices, and halal meat from animals slaughtered according to Islamic law; the Noori Insurance Agency and Zaki Traffic School, with business conducted in the languages of Afghanistan; the Nilare Boutique, featuring Afghan women's traditional finery; and the Cutting Edge Beauty salon, with a welcoming sign persuasively scripted in Afghan that sits next to a smaller placard reading SE HABLA ESPANOL.

Shortly after 9/11, Afghan merchants abandoned their bid for Little Kabul to be officially recognized by the Fremont city council—as U.S. troops first arrived in greater Kabul en route to defeating the Taliban. Yet Little Kabul still provides an irreplaceable opportunity for the Afghans who fled their country in the wake of the 1978 Soviet invasion to immerse themselves in the reinvigorating familiarity of language, food, and custom. In this sense, Little Kabul is also a reminder of loss—like Little Saigon, Koreatown, or the blocks of the Mission and Fruitvale Districts where merchants distinguish their storefronts with the names of the places they have left behind (Sinaloa Tacos, Jalisco Market, Guadalajara Restaurant) and burly young men affix the national flags of Mexico, El Salvador, or Guatemala to the rear windows of their four-by-fours.

Loss has always been central to the American story. One-third of the European immigrants who arrived in the United States during the great migrations of 1880 to 1924 returned to their countries of origin. But the presence of a Little Kabul can make life in America feel more accommodating and less chilly than it otherwise might. Little Kabul and the Bay Area's other immigrant enclaves provide a place for memory to thrive, a necessity for those bearing the weight of constant change. These recreations of the past serve as way stations for displaced people—even generations—passing slowly from one life to the next.

At Salang Pass—on Fremont Boulevard, down the street from American Dream Realty—Sunday diners arrive around three, and soon the English and Afghan languages both resound throughout the restaurant. The odd tourist completes the dining room roster, but it's largely Afghan families sprawled across the carpets at floor-level trays, eating all manner of kabob and heaping plates of quabili pallow, the national dish of lamb, raisins, carrots, and basmati rice seasoned with the ubiquitous cardamom. At the tables sit middle-aged couples and young Afghan women gathered in groups of three and four, dressed in black skirts and blouses—not the mandatory clothing once prescribed under the Taliban, but rather the mark of chic young Americans. The diners pick at bowls of homemade ice cream flavored with rosewater and topped with pistachios, and they drain great bowls of tea. Yet even amid the pleasures of delectable food consumed in comforting surroundings, Salang Pass suggests the persistence of loss.

On the far wall hangs a print of the famous "Afghan Girl," whose haunting, green-eyed gaze peered out from the folds of her ochre scarf in 1985, when she graced the cover of *National Geographic* magazine. Her name is Sharbat Gula, and she is a member of the Pashtun tribe, and quite literally the cover girl for the tragedy of her nation. Over the past quarter century, 1.5 million Afghans have lost their lives in continuing cycles of war, while 3.5 million have become refugees. When she was six, Sharbat Gula's parents were killed in a Soviet air raid. She fled to Pakistan, lived for years in the refugee camps, and returned home in the mid-1990s during a lull in the fighting, to a remote village without roads, schools, health facilities, or running water.

Nobody in Salang Pass even glances at the print of the Afghan girl. Her image is too familiar, even iconic; her story too terrible and ordinary. The question several diners ask the waiter instead concerns the music purring from the corner speakers. The song sounds familiar, but impossible to quite grasp above the heavy Middle Eastern bass drum beat and the whine of electric guitars. The waiter explains that it's something new, the marriage of a Spanish male singer and an Egyptian woman, and they are performing a mid-1960s hit from England, itself a reinvention of African American blues: the Animals' "Please Don't Let Me Be Misunderstood."

In a sense, the suburban sprawl of Fremont may provide the ideal circumstances for absorbing these contradictions. Centerville, the name of the district, is of course a misnomer: no center exists for the town of Fremont, whose tract homes and strip malls roll on placidly for over one hundred square miles. And without a physical center—no downtown, few architectural markers to stake down historical memory, and an endless procession of automobiles skating along a grid of wide streets and empty side-walks—Fremont may also be unusually prepared to accommodate the changes that have reshaped its culture over the past decade. In a fluid place, the new rapidly sinks its roots and claims territory as its own.

INDIA INDEPENDENCE DAY, Fremont

EGYPTIAN FESTIVAL, ST. ANTONIUS COPTIC ORTHODOX CHURCH, Hayward
Samia Mansour

Egyptian-born Emil Girgis, who is handing the basket of food to Samia Mansour, born in Cairo: "The first guy in 9/11, Mohammed Atta, he was Egyptian, so Americans blame Egyptians. When I say I'm Egyptian, Americans say, 'Oh, you are Muslim.' I say, 'No, I am Christian.' They say, 'We didn't know you have Christians there.'

"I came to this country July 16, 1977. In college I liked a Mexican woman and I ask her parents for her hand. They asked if I am Christian or Muslim, so I told them my Jesus is their Jesus is everybody's Jesus. We're married now for twenty-seven years, our children speak English, Spanish, and Arabic. My son is a sergeant in the Marine Corps, he went to Iraq nine months. We didn't have nothing to do with 9/11."

THE IRANIAN THERAPIST AND HER CAMBODIAN CLIENTS

DR. MONA AFARI STUDIED LAY'S IMPASSIVE EXPRESSION AS THE TRANSLATOR RENDERED HIS WORDS FROM Cambodian into English. "My mother and father," she heard the translator repeat, "...the Khmer Rouge take them. I never see again."

Mona watched Lay's eyes spark with pain as he recounted the story of his parents' murder, and she asked herself the question that had haunted her since founding the weekly therapy group: Could she—an Iranian-born, female therapist—breach the chasm separating her from these six middle-aged male survivors of the Cambodian holocaust and provide the help they desperately needed?

The Cambodian men had spilled into Oakland's largely Latino Fruitvale District like victims thrown from a terrible traffic accident—uneducated villagers battered physically and psychologically, utterly unprepared for life in America. In stark contrast, Mona was the upper class daughter of an Iranian industrialist, an educated urban cosmopolite, a Jew from a Muslim nation, and a willing immigrant to the United States.

Mona concentrated on the tone of Lay's voice. She did not understand the Cambodian language, but neither was she completely comfortable in English. She had grown up speaking Farsi—the only language that conveyed to her ears the deeper, wilder sea of feeling that churned beneath words. Lay spoke in a somber monotone about his long months shackled to fourteen other prisoners in an underground punishment cell, the terrible stench of the slop bucket, the weekly beatings that shattered his ribs—and how the soldiers pursued him in his nightmares, even now, two decades after leaving Cambodia.

Mona sat across from Lay, trying to imagine the full measure of his suffering, and she reminded herself that his story replicated, in similar horrific detail, that of each of the six men gathered around the small wooden table.

"I think, this morning," Mona announced, "we will all paint."

The translator repeated Mona's instructions and passed out sheets of cream-colored construction paper, brushes, and several sets of watercolors. The men busily daubed their canvasses with bright globs and streaks in a painterly routine that had grown familiar over the past nine months.

Mona had begun working with the Cambodians as a staff psychologist with the refugee program of Jewish Children's and Family Services—an effort founded originally to resettle Russian Jews. With the collapse of the Soviet Union, the stream of new arrivals slowed to a trickle and the Jewish refugee

Dr. Mona Afary with a Cambodian client

program faced a choice: close up shop, or offer its expertise to people from other backgrounds and faiths. The agency reached out to Muslims from Bosnia, Afghans fleeing their nation's civil war, and finally, the most traumatized people that Mona had encountered in twenty years as a psychotherapist, the Cambodians.

In the corner of the room, Mona's boom box thrummed a Chopin nocturne. She slowly circled around the table, stopping at last to inspect Lay's painting.

Lay had drawn a series of thatched brown huts nestled amid profuse greenery—his village back in Cambodia. At the far left border, he had inserted a volley of furious red slashes. Mona understood that the violent strokes indicated the approach of the Khmer Rouge and the end of everything in Lay's life that had promised peace, contentment, love, and hope.

Mona let escape a small, wistful sigh. This sense of foreboding and loss—it was her story, too. For twenty-five hundred years, her own family had lived in Iran. Yet as a Jew, she had always felt a stranger in her native country. In 1977, she moved to California to attend college. Two years later, from the safety of her new home, she received heartbreaking letters about the Islamic Revolution rapidly transforming Iran. Her friends were languishing in prison, enduring barbaric tortures, slated for the firing squads. Mona longed now to tell Lay and the other Cambodians about the tragedy of her own birthplace. Most of all, she wanted to convey that she, like them, still did not feel at home in America.

ON A WARM SATURDAY AFTERNOON IN APRIL, SOON AFTER THE FIRST BREAK OF SPRING, MONA DROVE TO Wat Dharmararam Buddhist temple in Stockton to celebrate the Cambodian New Year.

She arrived alone at the front gate of the temple grounds—a sprawling, nine-acre, plain-mowed field squeezed between several acres of strawberry patch and the area's recent swell of housing tracts. Once inside, Mona hesitated, feeling suddenly conspicuous and out of place among the crowd of one thousand Cambodians or more. Monks wearing sun-orange robes zigzagged along the pathway, their floor-length hems dragging in the dirt as they recited endless verses of Buddhist prayer. In the far corner, the fairgrounds loudspeaker boomed out shrill and unintelligible blessings.

Mona wandered across the temple grounds, not certain what direction to take. It felt strange to stand in the midst of such a large gathering of Cambodians—and yet most days, there was seldom a time when she did not find herself thinking about her Cambodian clients. Her agency's funding for the men's group had recently ended, but Mona continued to work with them, compelled by an urgency she found difficult to explain. She had even borrowed fifteen hundred dollars from her parents to subsidize her office rent. Mona told herself that people took out loans all the time to purchase a house or attend the university. For her, working with the Cambodians had become a similar necessity.

Within a few minutes, Mona spotted a familiar face—Lay, standing alongside some other men from her group and their families. They had all found seats on the picnic benches under a shade tree. Lay waved her toward the tables. Mona forced her face into a smile and ambled slowly in their direction.

She clapped Lay's extended hand between her two palms, squeezed, bowed, and smiled. Then she repeated the gesture with each of the men from her group and several of the women and children who stood alongside them. She wasn't certain which children belonged to whom, but she could see that everybody standing around the picnic tables knew who she was. Lay spoke rapidly in Cambodian, repeating Mona's name several times, causing each face in the crowd to turn toward her and appreciatively grin. One of the Cambodian women—tiny, wiry, perhaps fifty years old—opened a large picnic basket and began to ply Mona with treats. Mona pecked at her heaping plate of shrimp salad and sweet rice in coconut milk. When the woman handed her a steaming cup of lemongrass soup, Mona thought how familiar its sharp scent had become in recent months.

After eating, Mona thanked everybody profusely, backing away into the crowd as she waved good-bye. Lay stepped forward to shake her hand once again.

She knew that Lay trusted her; she was his only "American" friend. It didn't matter that he understood almost nothing about her background: few other Americans did either. In the center of the temple grounds, Mona recalled that when she first arrived in California, people confused Iran with Iraq; they thought Persians were Arabs. This kind of anonymity increased her remoteness, compounded her sadness. Only twenty years old when she left Iran, Mona had plunged into a deep depression. She had stopped eating, spent days in bed, withdrawn from college. Even now, years after fighting her way through her darkest, most immobilizing episodes, she still sometimes perceives the world to be lost in a haze. Mona thought of herself as someone who perpetually mislaid her glasses and could not quite bring life's contours and details into focus. The great benefit, gone unrecognized until now, was that this affliction gave her some idea of how the Cambodians viewed their own existence.

 Mona snaked a path along the busy walkway, straining to get her bearings as she peered over the sea of shoulders and heads. Soon she was caught in the irresistible drift of the crowd, and it delivered her to a story-high statue of a reclining Buddha. The sandstone figure sprawled across half the length of a basketball court, his eyes closed as though sleeping or dead. Mona had learned from the previous week's men's group that Cambodian New Year presents an opportunity to discard the year's sorrows and start over again. Alongside the reclining Buddha, a half-dozen children and adults doused one another with bowls of water tinted red, pink, and yellow—a playful ritual of washing away the past with a bright rinse of the future. A small round man about Lay's age laughed uproariously as his children soaked his starched white shirt and sharply creased black slacks.

Mona slipped out of the crowd and wound her way to the bandstand. A Cambodian pop band twanged electric guitars, while trap drums pounded out a rock-and-roll dance beat. Scores of Cambodian couples gyrated across the dance floor—the young men and women twirling and flailing their arms, amiably colliding with middle-aged couples primly executing a two-step. Mona saw in the faces of these dancers the sheer pleasure of belonging; they took for granted that whatever they had suffered in the past was understood by everybody in their midst. It was a feeling Mona rarely experienced.

She felt a hand clasp her wrist. It was the Cambodian woman she had met at Lay's picnic table, and she now pulled Mona onto the dance floor. Mona felt shy, frightened, slightly ridiculous. But she smiled graciously, throwing up her hands toward the sky in a facsimile of joyous abandon. Together she and the woman bobbled back and forth, locked together in no particular step as the guitars rang out and the drums pounded on.

In recent months, Mona had felt a change in her life. As a young woman, she had defined herself almost entirely in opposing terms—a Jew out of place in Muslim Iran, an Iranian lost in America. The hours, weeks, and months she had spent helping the Cambodians had put an end to this enduring discord and dissatisfaction. Mona knew that everything she'd given to the Cambodians had been handed back to her. In their company, she was even beginning to feel rooted in what had always been the cold soil of America. Sometimes Mona wondered: who was the healer and who was being healed?

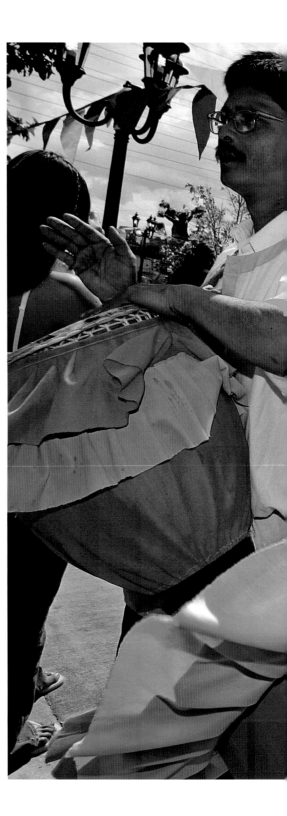

Cambodian New Year

CHINESE NEW YEAR, San Francisco

San Francisco's Chinese New Year Parade is now called the Southwest Airlines Chinese New Year Parade.

Laura Nieto is the advertising manager for Southwest Airlines: "Southwest Airlines has multicultural marketing strategies that target the African American segment, the Asian segment, and the Hispanic segment. We connect to the passion points of those communities so they'll get to know Southwest Airlines. In the Chinese New Year Parade, I see pride and determination, I see culture and color, I see vibrancy, I see passion—the same adjectives that apply to Southwest Airlines. Family, education, and love are important to the Asian community and to Southwest Airlines. So it makes sense for us to be a part of these cultural celebrations and events. We want all customers, regardless of their ethnic background, to fly Southwest Airlines—a provider of low-fare air travel."

83-year-old Afghanistan refugee Amir Mohammad Mehrdel, Fremont

SEPARATION, SPECTACLE, AND FORGETTING

N THE MIDST OF INTERMINGLING, WE LEAD SEPARATE LIVES.

When Fremont's city council changed the name of Hillside Drive to Gurdwara Road, in honor of the nearby Gurdwara Sahib Temple serving the area's growing population of Sikhs, some long-time residents complained that they could not pronounce the unfamiliar word. At a public meeting, a Sikh man rose to speak in favor of the change, observing that he couldn't pronounce the name of a Fremont main thoroughfare—Paseo Padre.

We can live side by side and disagree fundamentally about what we see around us, even the names we choose to describe our communities—perhaps an inevitability for a large and diverse society. But what does it signify to inhabit one of the most ethnically varied regions of the nation and not routinely interact in our neighborhoods and homes?

Circulate through the suburban and small-town streets of Pittsburg and Antioch in eastern Contra Costa County, or Hercules, El Sobrante, and San Pablo on the west side, and you'll find blacks, whites, Latinos, and Asians living next door to one another on block after block of tract homes—comprising, in fact, several of the most integrated census tracts in the state. Yet drive only a few miles, toward Lafayette or Livermore; or to the affluent enclaves across the San Mateo Bridge; or into Marin, one of the wealthiest counties in the nation—where 91 percent of adults possess at least a bachelor's degree—and you will have entered an area where it seems that the changes of the past three decades have been repealed and the bygone era of white dominion has somehow persisted.

Our paths may cross daily, or we can live in utter isolation from people whose differences are profound, confusing, and perhaps even frightening. And yet to judge by the number, variety, and persistence of public ethnic celebrations taking place throughout the Bay Area, it sometimes seems as though we are all acquainted on the most intimate terms.

Almost any day of the year, we can turn a corner and walk straight into one or another ethnic festival or parade, some commemoration built upon exact or contentious recollections of a key moment in the homeland's history, or the birthday of an indispensable man (almost always a man…) or simply the effusive declaration of a particular people that have managed against all odds to survive in this new country while retaining some aspect of language, culture, habit—or at least, a glimmer of memory.

The religious rituals and national festivities that once transpired within the insular realms of the family and community—those bulwarks against outside hostility, interference, and ignorance—are now ventilated with utmost confidence on the public stage.

Gathered upon the shores of San Francisco, Richmond, Sunnyvale, or Fremont, former citizens convene each year to celebrate the independence days of, among others, Brazil, Indonesia, Jamaica, Israel, Palestine, Chile, Korea, Finland, Nigeria, Pakistan, Peru, the Philippines, and Trinidad and Tobago. Hundreds of thousands of Bay Area residents ring in the new year with their alternatives to the first of January: the Vietnamese Tet festival in mid-April; the traditional Celtic celebration held on the last day of October; the Ukrainian commemoration (dated by the Julian calendar, instead of the Roman) in late January; not to mention Chinese, Hmong, Tibetan, Thai, and Cambodian observances, and the annual renewal ritual of the descendants of Mayans, whose Wajxakib Bat'z (literally, Eight Monkeys) celebration involves the destruction of old pottery, the shredding of fiber house mats, and the donning of new clothes amid incense and candlelight in San Francisco's Dolores Park.

Each year, Native Americans hold powwows in Davis, Turlock, Santa Clara, Martinez, at De Anza College and Stanford University—while Indigenous People's Day (Columbus Day to some) commences with a launch of small boats from both sides of the bay for a sunrise gathering on Alcatraz. The Bay Area is one of the few places in the world where residents can participate in both Croatian and Danish Mardi Gras; the Czech King Wenceslaus Festival and the English Queen's Ball; the birthdays of Peter Tosh and Mahatma Gandhi; and beery Middle European toasts to the months of October and May, the season of spring, and the reunification of Germany. The region hosts film festivals focused on Asian Americans, Native Americans, African Americans, Arabs, Basques, Italians, and Jews. Hawai'ian lu'aus occur in a dozen locations. The blessing of the fishing fleet begins each year with a procession through North Beach starting at Saints Peter and Paul Church, and the blessing of dogs, cats, rabbits, parrots, iguanas, and other beasts beloved by neighbors and parishioners takes place at San Francisco's Saint Boniface Church during the Feast of Saint Francis. In Irish pubs in Berkeley, Oakland, and San Francisco, devotees of the national literature celebrate June 16—Bloomsday, the day on which events unfold in James Joyce's *Ulysses*—with twenty-four-hour readings from the novel. On January 25, it's the Scots' turn with Burns Supper, in recognition of Robert Burns, their signatory poet.

What does this plethora of festivity say about life in the Bay Area today?

Most obviously, it shows that to glimpse the variety of the Bay Area's ethnic makeup, one need only step into the streets.

"Why don't we just stay quiet and keep our religion to ourselves?" asked Rabbi Yehudah Ferris, as he strummed an electric guitar after singing a rock version of "Chanukah O Chanukah" in front of Oakland's City Hall. "Because we're lamplighters. You might have forgotten your spirituality after so many years of melting into the melting pot. You just need a spark to access it."

He pointed the neck of his guitar toward the center of the plaza. "Look at Rabbi Kay dancing!" he cried. "His face shows unadulterated joy. He's whirling around like a dreidel. He's an extremely proper Englishman, he teaches Hebrew studies, he's a scholar, a genius. But when it comes to the holidays, he lets his hair down."

The traditions of the Bay Area's residents travel far beyond anyone's ability to appreciate, participate, understand, or even keep track of them. We are one and many, and the strain to resolve this essential contradiction—the incomplete reality of our national aspiration—is played out repeatedly in public commemoration. As the poet Walt Whitman reminded us over a hundred and fifty years ago: "The United States is not a nation, but a teeming nation of nations." Ethnic and religious festivals, rituals, and parades emphasize both the unbridgeable gap distinguishing cultures and the mere sliver of difference between one person and the next.

Yet while festivities often aim to protect the seed of national identity as it falls upon the rough ground of America, the effort can sometimes produce quite the opposite effect—altering the experience of participants in substantive ways, and even changing the celebrations themselves.

Dancing rabbis, Chanukah, Oakland City Hall

Kenneth Buncum lion dancing at the Saint Patrick's Day parade, San Francisco

Consider the annual Día de los Muertos, or Day of the Dead, a Mexican rite dedicated to the deceased and their visiting spirits. Today in San Francisco's Mission District, the Day of the Dead is less a somber Latino family ritual than a raucous interethnic party—a kind of art-school extravaganza, an urban Burning Man in black. In place of gathering around the grave sites of the departed, San Francisco's Day of the Dead revelers take to the streets in the company of stilt walkers and jugglers sporting Cat in the Hat headgear and body suits of luminous bones. The sounds of the holiday include the blare of a Mexican brass band, but also the rumble of African percussion, the metallic ping of Trinidad steel drums, a Brazilian sordo banging the bass drum beat, congas, Andean flutes, and a soprano sax spinning solos for the pleasure of young dancers who twirl in giddy circles as though at a rave instead of a public wake. At Garfield Park, where the Day of the Dead concludes its street parade, the spirit of Mexican Catholicism cedes space to the multicultural New Age in a bewitching and painstakingly crafted array of altars designed with a countercultural twist: a tree full of sheep skulls acknowledging the victims of pollution; a wooden tray arrayed with photos of Afghan children, plastic toy soldiers, and cards drawn from the tarot, all dedicated to the victims of war. Each year, the crowd includes more white, Asian, and black faces; proportionately fewer Latinos. It's all distinctively San Franciscan, not quite as it started, but vital and absorbent, alive and adaptive.

Or take that most American and long-lived of ethnic celebrations, the Saint Patrick's Day parade.

One hundred years ago, the Irish ranked as the Bay Area's largest foreign-born group, with working class families occupying whole neighborhoods south of Market in San Francisco and across the bay in west Berkeley. On Saint Patrick's Day, they assembled in defiant opposition to the lingering anti-Catholic and anti-Irish tenor of frontier San Francisco. Irish muscle had laid the tracks for the continental railway, the cable cars and Key system trains. Irish labor had built the city's houses and commercial structures and then, after the 1906 earthquake and fire, rebuilt them. Saint Patrick's Day acknowledged Irish strength in numbers and a growing confidence in achievement: We are here, firmly planted, and indispensable.

Today San Francisco is far less Irish in every aspect (though Bay Area immigrants from Ireland and the United Kingdom rank only slightly behind Korea and ahead of Guatemala and Iran). But the large and boisterous Saint Patrick's Day parade down Market Street continues to assert an indissoluble Irish grain in the mix of the city's cultural life. It's just that now the mix is spiked with other people, rituals, costumes, and customs having nothing to do with nostalgia for the Emerald Isle.

As the parade winds to its conclusion, thousands of observers cheer the sinuous prance and fierce bucking of the Chinese lion dancers, an Asian complement to the Celtic festival. The presence of the dancers fails to elicit the crowd's surprise—even when the lead dancer slips out from under the huge lion's head and turns out to be a black teenager. "Any culture can join in," explained seventeen-year-old Kenneth Buncum, who took up lion dancing in sixth grade with the encouragement of his best friend's immigrant Chinese family. "It's like I'm part of the Chinese culture," said Buncum, "but I don't do other Chinese things. Nobody's had a problem with it. Nobody ever says anything to me. Nobody even sees it as unusual."

More to the point, the fact that Chinese lion dancers—Asian or black—can today weave effortlessly through an Irish celebration, welcomed and even celebrated for the gift of their own presence, speaks to the fact that many public events also serve as festivals of forgetting—momentary annulments of hostilities, grievances, and even tradition itself. In the late nineteenth century, the completion of the transcontinental railroad left Irish and Chinese rail workers unemployed and competing for scarce jobs. Immigrant Irish politicians soon led the charge for restrictions on Asian immigration, and restive crowds of young thugs periodically sacked Chinatown. Today this old rivalry fails to manifest, even on the sidelines of the city's annual Saint Patrick's Day celebration.

BHANGRA AEROBICS, San Francisco

Bhangra is a traditional Punjabi harvest dance based on the labor of plowing and sowing. In the Bay Area, bhangra has become a trendy exercise for non-Indians in gyms and health clubs. Called an MBW—Masala Bhangra Workout—it's an alternative to the tedium of aerobics.

Vicki Virk, a San Francisco lawyer born in Punjab, India, teaches bhangra aerobics at Crush gym: "The farmers who originated bhangra worked hard at digging, chopping crops, a lot of arm movements and bending, so they were in great shape. When you dance bhangra, you move your body fast from head to toe, so it's become an aerobics thing here. It's ironic, though, because most people at the gym just hear the beat and dance to it. They have no idea about Punjab, farming, or dancing with joy after you sell your crops. A lot of Punjabi people in the U.S. don't want to see bhangra danced like this, because it takes the meaning away. But I think it's important to share our culture, because so many Americans think they're on their own little planet. I tell my students that bhangra has a history. So it makes them curious to know—where is Punjab, what do people do there?"

METROPOLITAN COMMUNITY CHURCH, San Francisco

The Metropolitan Community Church holds a Christian service on Sundays and a Buddhist service on Mondays.

Ji-Sing Norman Eng, Minister of Buddhist Spirituality at the Metropolitan Community Church: "We're not trying to mesh religions. A lot of Christians are making a commitment to practice meditation and mindfulness in their personal life, to supplement their Christian faith. We're grounded in the jewels of our ancestors, but we allow for the mystery of the unexpected."

PROCESSION OF *LA VIRGEN DE GUADALUPE*, San Francisco

On December 12, Bay Area worshippers of la Virgen de Guadalupe reenact the story of Juan Diego, the six-teenth-century Aztec peasant who was visited by the spirit of the Virgin Mary—only to be turned away at the door to his church by a Mexican priest who doubted his story. Over the years in San Francisco, a dozen men and women costumed as Aztecs have danced in procession toward St. Mary's Cathedral. And on each occasion a Mexican American priest stood at the church door and refused the "pagans" entry. "He brought all his prejudices from Mexico with him," said Pedro García, a Mexican immigrant who initiated the pro-cession. "It gave me such shame. We prayed for a miracle."

The miracle came in the form of an Irish American priest who took over when the Mexican-born priest moved on. Knowing nothing about the controversy, the new priest turned to Pedro for guidance as the Aztec dancers approached. "They should come in," said Pedro, with a shrug and the barest glimpse of a smile. "There is no conflict with the Aztecs. We are all one to la Virgen."

Facing page: DECEMBER 12, *DÍA DE LA VIRGEN DE GUADALUPE*, MISSION DISTRICT, San Francisco

Aztec dancers on the street, denied entry to the church

PCHUM BEN, THE CAMBODIAN FESTIVAL OF THE DEAD, San Jose

During an annual fifteen-day ceremony to honor the spirits of the dead, Cambodian Buddhist monks bless and eat food brought by families as offerings to their hungry ancestors. The ceremony gained additional significance following the murder of 1.7 million Cambodians by the Khmer Rouge from 1975 to 1979. In San Jose, Cambodian refugees celebrate the full rituals of Pchum Ben, while in Cambodia there have been moves by economic advisors to curtail the celebrations.

From the Phnom Penh Post, *October 21, 2001: "The International Financial Fund and the Global Bank are distressed…by Cambodia's failure to adapt its cultural traditions to modern conditions…With the country's labor force rising in the early hours to take offerings to departed ancestors, there must be an enormous decline in labor productivity…Cambodia cannot afford such an annual blow to its ability to compete in this era of globalization…In most Western developed countries, communion with the dead is restricted to one night per year, known as Halloween…This means that Cambodia is spending at least fourteen times as much time as necessary in appeasing its ghosts…Cambodian ghosts…may well feel offended by a shift to a one-day observance. However…Cambodian ghosts are no less patriotic than their counterparts in the developed countries, and can be counted on to make this sacrifice in the national interest."*

INDIGENOUS PEOPLE'S DAY, Berkeley
Anjelica and Felicia Sanchez

Susie Pinola is the girls' grandmother: "They're full-blooded California Indian girls. But you wouldn't know it unless you asked them. They're the only Native American girls at their school. I keep telling them, it's okay to be Indian, these days it's okay. They don't know the Pomo language, but they're hungry for stories of the old times. A long time ago their headbands would have been buckskin, but this is contemporary, this is now. The abalone and beads cover their eyes so they aren't looking at the boys. It was them that asked their Grandpa Lanny to teach them to dance. We showed them the moves, then they were on their own."

FROM THE PEAK OF OAKLAND'S MOUNTAIN VIEW CEMETERY, THE VIEW of the Bay Area cuts across time as well as distance.

The most pleasing view of the cemetery itself has always been Millionaire's Row, the nineteenth-century array of obelisks, pyramids, domes, sarcophagi, and hillside mausoleums erected as the final mansions for Bay Area commercial barons descended from European immigrants. But the most striking feature of the cemetery is the speed with which people from all parts of the world begin to mingle once they have departed the realm of the living. Along the central slope winding its way up toward Millionaire's Row, the modest grave of Gustav Johnson of Finland is situated near Tsuna Nakayama of Japan. The Chang, Huang, and Fong families have found a place for themselves among the gravesites of the Brauns, Pettits, and Lightenthalers.

Established in 1865, the Mountain View Cemetery initially reflected the Bay Area's Anglo bias in commemorative design, with flocks of Victorian marble angels keeping watch at mausoleum gates or weeping amid a field of granite lambs and cherubs marking the graves of children. Today you find far different symbols of respect for the dead in the stones sitting atop Jewish grave markers and the tangerines and oranges balancing upon Asian headstones. Even the trees shading the dead suggest the general mix taking place below the graveyard, among the living—Mexican palms and Chilean monkey puzzle trees sprout among Australian eucalyptus and Japanese maple, as Italian stone pines and Chinese bamboo align with live oaks and coastal redwoods.

At Hillside Gardens, across the bay in Colma, the prospective purchasers of gravesites employ feng shui, the ancient Chinese practice of arranging surroundings to attract positive energy—thereby guaranteeing that entire families will rest in locations of optimal peace. In funeral homes from Fremont to Vallejo, Hindu mourners wash their deceased with honey and yogurt in preparation for cremation, while the Vietnamese burn artificial paper money to be carried into the afterlife, with the ashes deposited in pots specially provided by the mortuary. Cemeteries throughout the Bay Area now host ceremonies for Día de los Muertos and Ching Ming, the Chinese ritual that involves cleaning the headstone, weeding the grounds, and offering a whole steamed chicken, roast pork, or selected dim sum (along with chopsticks and wine cups) to the spirits of the dead. In Oakland, Stockton, and San Jose, the

Cambodian community celebrates Pchum Ben in recollection of the dead—presided over by the few Buddhist monks who managed to survive the Khmer Rouge and find their way to America.

These varied last rites also suggest the interplay of religious traditions so prominent throughout the Bay Area. Whereas Sunday has for decades been rightly characterized as "the most segregated day of the week," the truth today is more complex. Religion now plays the dual role of sustaining distinct ethnic communities even as it draws together unlikely congregations from other races and backgrounds—often transforming religious practices in the process. Even when color, class, language, and history appear to be barriers to mutual sympathy and recognition, belief may bind together disparate peoples.

Mountain View Cemetery,
Oakland

Day of the Dead, Oakland Museum of California

SOKA GAKKAI, Oakland
Sylviaette Hill, Tokunbo Adeyemi, Molaundo Jones

A LIFE OF BUDDHISM AND BLACKNESS

DIANE CHEATUM SAT IN THE FRONT ROW OF THE SOKA GAKKAI COMMUNITY CENTER IN EL CERRITO, HER eyes focused on a three-foot-high mahogany cabinet positioned at the center of the altar. Behind the cabinet's closed doors hung the Gohonzon, a parchment scroll inscribed with the Lotus Sutra, Soka Gakkai's sacred text. "Look deeply into the Gohonzon," thought Diane, drawing upon the lesson she had absorbed over twenty-five years of Buddhist practice, "and what you'll find there is yourself." In her mind's eye, Diane saw with utter clarity a sixty-year-old chestnut-brown black woman, her shoulders slumped forward upon her small round frame—her heart breaking as she struggled to make it through the hardest day of her life.

In the row directly behind Diane, her niece Veronica started to sob and then erupted into wails.

Diane whipped around sharply and scowled.

"Hush!" she ordered Veronica, her deep voice full of gravel. "If I don't act the fool, you can't act a fool. This is my son."

Diane returned to face the altar, trying to calm her breathing. She knew how much Tony had meant to Veronica. They'd been twin coons, Diane liked to say, drawing on the Louisiana country slang of her parents. Veronica still didn't understand why Diane was determined to lay Tony to his final rest this Saturday afternoon with a Buddhist ritual instead of the Christian burial common to their family. Veronica was baffled by Diane's Buddhism. Black people simply were not Buddhists; they worshipped as Baptists, Catholics, Pentecostals. Buddhism was an Asian religion, perhaps of interest to some white folks; but it had nothing to do with being black.

In truth, Soka Gakkai is the nation's largest Buddhist organization and its most racially diverse—as the array of black, white, Asian, and Latino faces scattered throughout the meeting hall in nearly equal numbers could attest. Yet until today, none of Diane's family had ever set foot inside her place of worship.

Diane's impatience with her niece subsided, her breathing relaxed. She turned to steal a long, uncertain look at the hall's thirty rows of wooden benches filling up with mourners.

Her thirty-eight-year-old son, Tony, had died suddenly from a drug overdose, concluding a two-decade-long blur of crack cocaine addiction, drinking, jail time, and finally, confinement in a psychiatric institution. A few weeks before he died, Tony started telephoning family members everyday, sometimes two or three times—always talking, talking, wearing them out. Diane's sister labeled him "a loving pest."

Diane's one great wish, always to be disappointed, had been that Tony would take up the Buddhist chanting practice that had transformed her own life. Maybe he would do so in his next incarnation, she now told herself. For twenty-five years, Diane had twice daily chanted *Nam Myoho Renge Kyo*, Soka Gakkai's essential ritual. She hoped her devotion might allow Tony's soul to be reborn somewhere in the world within a Buddhist household. It was a difficult concept to convey to her family of African American Christians.

Veronica had ceased crying and now sat behind Diane in tightly held silence. At Veronica's side was Diane's older sister, Lola, her mouth drawn in an expression of perplexity as she tried to make sense of the Gohonzon cabinet sitting upon the altar. Flanking Lola sat Aunt Melba, up from New Orleans, fidgeting madly with her handbag, her eyes darting nervously about the room, obviously distressed about whatever would happen next—and behind her, nearly three dozen other family members clad in their somber black burying dresses and Sunday service charcoal suits. Surrounding Diane's family sat eighty members of Soka Gakkai—Buddhists of every color.

"I am the only person who can get us all through this day," thought Diane as she surveyed the crowd. "Because despite what anybody else thinks, I am a Buddhist and I am a strong black woman."

SADAKU PLACED TWO SLENDER GLASS VASES OF WHITE CHRYSANTHEMUMS ON EITHER SIDE OF THE ALTAR. She was Diane's closest friend, one of the Japanese women whose quiet, insistent devotion to daily chanting served as the backbone of Soka Gakkai. For many African American converts, including Diane, the Japanese women who had arrived in the United States during the 1950s as the brides of American servicemen—many of them black—proved the perfect emissaries for an unfamiliar religion.

"I wouldn't have heard nothing white people said about Buddhism," Diane admitted. "I'd have put up a barrier the moment they opened their mouths. But those little Japanese women—man, my heart just opened."

Throughout the Bay Area's poor and working class neighborhoods, the Japanese women had approached strangers on street corners, evangelizing with passionate conviction about the teachings of a thirteenth-century Japanese monk who preached an egalitarian faith among the poor. The women became fixtures in San Francisco's predominantly black Bayview District and along Market Street, promising in their imperfect English a happier life to anyone who would accompany them to a meeting and learn to chant. Diane felt an intensely personal connection to these women, sensing similarities in their experiences and her own. As new arrivals in America, they were often treated with coldness, indifference, even hostility—just what Diane felt when dealing with the white world.

As the doors of the meeting hall closed, Diane felt the eyes of the entire room settle upon her. She had dressed for Tony's memorial with dignified simplicity, wearing a crisply pressed pair of tan trousers and a plain white silk blouse. Around her neck, as always, she had strung a four-inch-long ceramic ankh. Shaped like a thick T with a small loop at the top, the ankh is an ancient Egyptian symbol of eternal life. Diane's right hand now reached for the ankh, and she fingered it nervously. On occasions when people—particularly black people—mistook the ankh for a Christian cross, Diane corrected them sharply. The ankh stood for Africa, the cradle of humanity, black people's link to their beginnings.

Diane now stared at the altar where Tony's ashes lay.

The service commenced as a young Japanese woman struck a foot-long silver chime with a wooden mallet. Its shrill metallic ping washed over the room, gradually dissipating. In complete silence, a slender, middle-aged white man paced up the center aisle and turned to face the gathering. Twenty-five years ago, before Buddhism, Diane could never have tolerated or even imagined sitting in a family funeral in the company of white people. But earlier that week, she had selected Jim Leach—"this beautiful white guy"—to lead the afternoon's service. "When I'm being real with Buddhism," Diane had explained to her family upon making the decision, "it doesn't matter if it's black or white. If you can get to the level of Buddhahood to understand the importance of all human life, then you can't be prejudiced." And then she drew her face into a frown and shrugged. "I ain't there yet."

Unexpectedly, Jim's first instructions at the service confused Diane's family in a way that had nothing to do with race.

"Please, come up to the altar," Jim asked, "and dip your hands into the ashes."

On the bench behind Diane, Aunt Melba emitted a small, feral shriek.

"Those ashes," Melba whispered loudly to Veronica, "are Tony!"

Veronica rose to her feet, planning to flee, appalled by the notion of sinking her hands into her beloved cousin's remains.

Diane turned to her family and patiently calmed them, explaining that the Buddhist funeral ritual always included a reminder of death's proximity—an echo, they might recall, of the Christian admonition about dust to dust. The ashes used in the ritual came from charred paper and wood. Tony's ashes lay upon the altar, unmolested.

Several dozen Buddhists streamed out of the pews and walked to the front of the room to dip their hands into a large ceramic bowl containing the ashes. Veronica and Melba remained in their seats.

Another strike of the silver chime flooded the room.

At the front of the hall, Jim drew his hands together in a figure of prayer, and delivered a quick bow to the roomful of Buddhists. Then he lowered his head to Diane with a deeper and more intimate genuflection. Behind him on the altar sat the Gohonzon, still locked behind its cabinet doors. Jim opened each door and stepped to the side. The inky black lettering sprang forward in vivid contrast to the white parchment upon which it was embossed.

In the front row, Diane drew her fingertips together and began to chant, her words flowing into the stream of voices rising up from behind.

Nam Myoho Renge Kyo, Nam Myoho Renge Kyo, Nam Myoho Renge Kyo...

The room resounded with the basso hum of four barely intelligible words, eighty voices braided together in wavering harmony. *Nam Myoho Renge Kyo, Nam Myoho Renge Kyo...*With Diane's sonorous baritone blended hoarsely into the mix, wheezing and pleading from the front row, the chant resembled the low steady grind of a huge electric motor. Occasionally, the chant tumbled ahead of itself with a spurt of off-key enthusiasm. Then the chanters slowed down, recapturing the rhythm, gently drifting into a placid stream of ever present sound.

Diane produced a string of black plastic prayer beads from her trousers' front pocket. She energetically worried each bead, her fingers nimbly sorting as she squeezed out each syllable of chant in prolonged susurration. The hall vibrated and buzzed, the sound ceaseless, driven by a studious and ethereal energy.

In the row behind Diane, Lola rocked her head in rhythm to the chant, transported by sound. It was like being in church, she told herself, the invocation and presence of something greater than the sum of all voices—the noise of heaven swinging open up its heavy gates to the kingdom. She hummed along, as though the chant was a familiar hymn—"Old Rugged Cross" or "Amazing Grace." Scattered along the wooden benches like hymnals were transliterations of the chant rendered syllable by syllable into English. Lola picked up a copy.

After a half-hour, the chanting ended with a final flush of sound, the last syllable concluding like a slammed door. And then utter silence. Jim nodded to Diane. Veronica, Lola, and all the rest of her family stared at her, wondering but no longer worrying about what would come next. Diane rose from the front row and trod a deliberate path to the podium. At the side of the altar, she breathed deeply until she felt a wave of calm roll through her body—and then a jolt of joy. Tony was with her. She felt him closer than any time since he was a little boy. She peered across the room, her gaze falling upon her family. Her lips pursed slightly, and she thought, "I gotcha! I finally got you all here."

Diane held a single sheaf of paper, and she slowly waved it over her head like a piece of vital news everyone in the room must see—a letter from the departed.

"I want to read this in honor of Tony." She paused, steadying herself. "It's from Nelson Mandela's inaugural speech as the first black president of South Africa."

Diane allowed a single beat to pass, a moment of expectant silence.

"'Our deepest fear,'" intoned Diane, her hands gripping either side of the podium, "'is not that we are inadequate. Our deepest fear is that we are powerful beyond measure...We were born to make manifest the glory of God that is within us. It's not just in some of us. It's in everyone...'"

Another black woman in Soka Gakkai had sent Diane the speech. She had heard about Tony's death, and she knew of Diane's consuming interest in Africa. Diane now read the rest of the speech very slowly, determined that everyone in the hall should grasp its message.

Diane's friend Sadaku had once told her that a beginning Buddhist is like an old garden hose left out all winter. Diane should expect to see a great deal of dirt and muck come tumbling forward before anything clear and pleasing burst forth. Diane felt that purity now.

The Mandela speech seemed precisely the right way to conclude Tony's memorial. Just as the Japanese women had been for Diane the ideal emissaries for Buddhism, so now did Mandela faultlessly convey the message of complicated, paradoxical unity that gave shape and direction to Diane's life. We are all alone in our separate skins of many colors—and we all belong to the single body of humanity. Mandela understood this truth. In Buddhist terms, he exemplified the possibilities of compassion, forgiveness, and grace—even in the face of death.

At the ceremony's conclusion, Diane's family and her Buddhist friends swarmed around her, praising the speech, requesting copies. Yet the speech bears a more complicated provenance than anyone inside the hall realized.

Although the words Diane recited at her son's memorial are commonly attributed to Nelson Mandela, they do not appear in his 1994 inaugural. The passage she cited actually comes from a book entitled *Return to Love*, published in 1992 by Marianne Williamson—a white American of Jewish origins, a New Age interpreter of the Christian text *A Course in Miracles*.

Yet standing at the podium with all the people she loved spread before her to bear witness, the origins of the speech could not have mattered less. What Diane felt most powerfully was the sensation of her two worlds merging—the corresponding halves of American Buddhism and African American blackness joined together to make a whole.

Diane Cheatum, Oakland

THE UNDERGROUND, Oakland
Afia Walking Tree and members of the Underground Drum Sanctuary

In Oakland, Jamaica-born Afia Walking Tree started a school for African drumming called Spirit Drumz. She encourages women of all races to drum with her.

Afia Walking Tree: "When white women, black women, and all women drum together, we're having a conversation—how do we walk together? If you're drumming and you don't have feelings come up around race or class or privilege, whether you're a Latina, American Indian, Asian, black, or white woman—you're not feeling. I started Spirit Drumz to heal that—and then the whole stuff about racism showed up. A woman of African descent said, 'Look, I don't want to drum with white people.'

Shawn Nealy, an African American drummer: "It's no disrespect to tell white women there are times we just want to drum with black women—to talk amongst our own people. But our purpose is to awaken all people, so it's also crucial to have different ethnic groups at the table. If they begin to understand their own history as well as ours, they will begin to appreciate the drums—not with guilt but with compassion and respect. So anyone who's willing to drum with us truthfully and authentically is more than welcome."

Laurie McWhorter, a white drummer of English, Irish, German, Swiss background: "Some women of African heritage said it's really hard to be drumming with white women. There's so much hurt and pain and fear. I got to the place of giving the drums up—forget it, I'm going to learn an Irish drum. And then I thought, 'Chicken, you need to be doing these drums.' Me being in white skin playing African drums gives us an opportunity to talk about racism. To leave would be to give up."

"WHAT, THEN, IS THE AMERICAN," ASKED HECTOR ST. JEAN DE Crevecoeur some two hundred and twenty years ago, "this new man?"

Crevecoeur's famous question echoes through the entirety of American history, seizing upon the fact that our nation remains a perpetual work in progress.

What is an American?

When Kal Phan first stepped off the plane from the Thai refugee camp where he had spent his childhood, he couldn't begin to answer this question. Nor could he have imagined that his arrival in this country, along with thousands of other Mien fleeing Laos after the Vietnam War, would help propel America toward its next phase of reinvention.

The first Americans Kal had seen as a child in Laos were CIA operatives charged with enlisting members of his village to fight the communist insurgents. To a man, the CIA had been white. To Kal, along with everybody else in his village, American meant Caucasian.

"The biggest shock when I came to this country was seeing black people," he remembered. "We couldn't make any sense of it. What are they, and how come they're so different? We didn't even have a word for them in the Mien language."

Kal's family eventually settled in a Richmond neighborhood filled with people of every race. "It was very difficult," he acknowledged, "for Mien people to understand that 'American' referred to anyone living here, including Asian, Caucasian, Latino, or African American." But the cultural confusion cut both ways. Kal also found that Americans mistook the Mien for the Chinese or Japanese, and he was often regarded as a kind of undifferentiated Asian anybody.

"Most frustrating," said Kal, "is explaining over and over to other Asians who the Mien are. Chinese, Japanese, Korean, Thai—they know *nothing* about the Mien. So we have to explain who the Mien are and why we are here…to every person we meet. We get so frustrated!"

In a final unintentional insult, the few people Kal did encounter who had heard about the Laotian hill tribes tended to mistake the Mien for the Hmong, who outnumbered the Mien in America a hundredfold. "The Mien were a minority in Laos," he said. "Here in the Bay Area, we are a minority within a minority within a minority."

Today Kal works as an administrator at Richmond High School. The student body is half Latino, with the remainder almost equally divided between blacks and Asians, including over one hundred Mien. "But the primary language of many Mien kids," he pointed out, "is Ebonics."

What are you?

It's the signal question of a multicultural era, and while some equally bear the weight of curiosity and ignorance, others bristle at the unflattering implications: what are you; not who. Yet questions about origins seem inevitable. Throughout California, more than one million people claim descent from at least two races. At UC Berkeley, nearly a quarter of the students polled in 2004 identified themselves as "multi-racial or multi-ethnic." With time, the share of multi-race Californians will grow even larger as the children of immigrants marry in greater numbers outside their respective communities.

Yet life in a dynamic and sometimes combustibly multicultural region brings with it opportunities and imperatives that render identity even more complicated. We pursue multiple lives, propelled by circumstance and design through an array of daily encounters that introduce us to new music, food, languages, religions, and suppositions about the way the world works and our rightful place in it. We bow to the influences or we back away. Most often, we remain unaware of the multiplicity of ways in which the people surrounding us also shape us. And in time, we find that our lives have crystallized into assemblages of identities, some related to ethnicity or culture, and others utterly incidental.

Kal Phan is Mien and American. A member of a preliterate hill tribe from Laos and the first Mien refugee to earn a Ph.D. from UC Berkeley. As someone in his forties—a member of the Mien's "middle generation"—Kal is often called upon to resolve differences between elders, who still recall the war that forced them to leave Laos, and today's teenagers, who foment their own local violence within Southeast Asian street gangs. Kal helped organize the Bay Area's first Mien Olympics—a striking accomplishment within a culture that does not traditionally participate in competitive sports. He is also a fanatical fan of volleyball.

Who can keep track of which identity predominates from day to day, from hour to hour?

Most decisively and intimately, we change the direction of our lives—and the shape of society—by the people we marry and the children we bring into the world.

Oeum Loch grew up in West Oakland following her family's flight from Cambodia. During adolescence, she cultivated as friends the black kids she encountered each day along Market and 16th Streets. When a high school acquaintance introduced her to Michael Corbett, a young black man from Los Angeles whose Spanish-speaking mother came from Panama, she could see no cultural barriers that should prevent them from marrying. Blacks and Latinos had always been a part of her life.

Although Oeum had grown up hearing tales about Cambodia from her parents, it was Michael's growing interest in her family's history that led the couple to visit the country. "Michael bought tons of books on Pol Pot, the Khmer Rouge regime, the sex trade going on now. For the first time," recalled Oeum, "I felt that I needed to go there."

When Oeum returned to Oakland, she found that her role in the Cambodian community had profoundly altered. She was greeted as somebody important bearing vital news of the homeland. Having successfully negotiated the boundaries between being a dutiful Cambodian daughter and an independent young American, she began working as a translator for the community's elders, assisting them with the perennially confounding aspects of their new home. Michael's embrace of Oeum's background had changed her more than him.

Then the couple's daughter was born. "We called her Nina," said Oeum, "because it sounded Cambodian, Spanish, and also Japanese"—a language both she and Michael had studied. The child unexpectedly aided her husband's integration into a small corner of the local black community.

For two and a half years, Michael had been going to a barbershop in Oakland's flatlands off High Street, once an entirely black neighborhood now ceding room to immigrant Latino and Asian families. The clientele was young, the barbers all black men in their twenties, and the talk involving music, cars, women, and life in the neighborhood seldom included him. "I'm not street," said Michael, noting that his speech, style, and attitudes come straight out of the black middle class. One afternoon, Michael brought Nina into the barbershop and introduced her to the crew.

"Hey, man," asked one of the young barbers. "What's your daughter mixed with?"

"I said, 'She's part Cambodian.' And the barber goes, 'Oh yeah, my daughter's mixed too. She's half Chinese.' Now this barber talks to me all the time. My mixed daughter's what made the difference."

CROATIAN MARKO POLO DAY, San Francisco.

Janusz Zelazny of the Lowiczanie Polish Folk Ensemble explains, "We came to help the Croatian community celebrate their favorite son, Marko Polo. But we are from the proud and distinct Cieszyn region of Poland. We are not Croatian."

THIRTY-SEVENTH ANNUAL SAN FRANCISCO FESTIVAL OF THE CHARIOTS
INTERNATIONAL SOCIETY FOR KRISHNA CONSCIOUSNESS, San Francisco
Krishna Prema das

Krishna Prema das: "I was a lecturer in philosophy in Uganda, then came to Wisconsin to do my doctoral thesis in linguistics, but I found Lord Krishna. There are no different races or skin colors in Krishna consciousness—we laugh at all classifications and pigeonholes because the body is just a temporary shell. When people wonder about a black devotee of Krishna, I tell them you never know what you're going to be in the next life, so you should have some humility."

Facing page: *Mother's Day Celebration, Berkeley*

Anthony Brown

THE AMERICAN RHAPSODIES OF ANTHONY BROWN

WHEN THE MEMBERS OF ANTHONY BROWN'S ASIAN AMERICAN ORCHESTRA FILED INTO COAST RECORDERS early in the morning to rehearse *American Rhapsodies*—a reinterpretation of George Gershwin's masterpiece, *Rhapsody in Blue*—they immediately pushed the studio's serviceable upright piano into a corner and tossed their leather jackets on top. Although Gershwin's composition ranks as the most familiar piano concert piece in the American repertoire, the instrument played no role—except as a clothes rack—in the orchestra's updated recording. Where the piano had stood, bandleader Anthony Brown instead rolled into place an enormous metal gong.

"First," instructed Anthony, leafing through the score as he swiveled on the stool behind his trap drums to face the orchestra, "the gong. Then the *yangqins*."

Anthony counted out the downbeat and bashed the gong. Then he pointed to the Zhao sisters sitting in a tiny glass-enclosed booth in the far corner. Poised above the wide wooden trapezoidal base of their twin *yangqins*, or Chinese hammered dulcimers, the two women rapidly beat the instruments' steel strings with a pair of light, wooden, leather-tipped sticks. Isolated from the rest of the orchestra, the instruments' sound suggested a profuse scattering of metallic ants, a percolation up and down the wiry middle register—a twenty-first-century substitute for the piano's conventional statement of the theme.

"Whoa!" shouted Anthony, clapping his hands following the final dispersion of notes. "We're definitely not in the Western Hemisphere anymore." He beamed, gazing at the *yangqins*, and then his eyes roved across the room to fall on the *sheng*, a Chinese mouth organ equipped with seventeen pipes and a bowl-like chamber braced in the palms of the hand, and the two-foot-long wooden Japanese flute called a *shakuhachi*. "I don't think anybody's heard these voicings before. And we're talking about a piece," he said, "that's been an inextricable part of the American fabric for eighty years."

The inspiration for *Rhapsody in Blue* first struck George Gershwin in January 1924, as he rode the commuter train from New York to Boston. On his journey, the composer perceived in the railroad's "steely rhythms, its rattlety-bang" an evocation of the new America then being riveted together from the European immigrant enclaves of the large eastern cities and black migrants streaming in from the rural South. Within a week of his return to New York, Gershwin completed *Rhapsody*'s rough draft. "I heard it as a sort of musical kaleidoscope of America," he later declared, "of our vast melting pot, of our incomparable national pep, our blues, our metropolitan madness."

The following month, Gershwin premiered *Rhapsody* on Abraham Lincoln's centennial birthday, intending the music to stand as a progressive statement about American race relations. He had appropriated the musical languages he knew best—the European concert repertoire, Jewish folk melodies, the popular songs of Tin Pan Alley, and most critically, African American blues and jazz—and forged a composition whose exhilarating freshness owed everything to the blend of its sources. From the opening strains of a lone clarinet's plaintive moan—an off-key blare of Eastern European klezmer resolving into the blues—*Rhapsody* asserted that American music was as fundamentally hybrid as its people.

Eighty years later, Anthony Brown concluded that America's changing ethnic mix called for an expansive reinterpretation of Gershwin's composition.

"*Rhapsody in Blue* was a reflection of Manhattan in the early 1920s," explained Anthony, as several musicians required for the next section wove their way through the vines of microphones suspended from the ceiling and took their seats. "It's important," he said, "that Americans from all backgrounds hear themselves reflected in this score today."

Anthony's arrangement features fifteen performers doubling on forty-five different instruments—eight fewer players than the original orchestra now charged with handling almost twice as many instruments. In an effort to evoke "the full palette of America," Anthony filled his band with musicians adept not only on the brass and woodwinds of a conventional Western orchestra—but also the Chinese violin, viola, and reed trumpet; Japanese flutes and drums; percussion from Cuba, Africa, China, and Japan; and steel drums from Trinidad. "In order to realize this project," he explained, "I had to find the right people to carry it off—musicians who have fluency in a variety of traditions, who are cultural polyglots."

Anthony moved to the podium at the center of the studio, puzzling over the score and frowning to himself. The first take sounded crisp and clean, but he was aiming for a performance equal in power to the exuberant violations he had introduced into Gershwin's original. His eyes tightened as he cued the brass section and then the Chinese violin, and this time the band soared even higher and wilder than before.

"THERE'S NO OTHER MUSIC THAT SOUNDS LIKE THIS," DECLARED ANTHONY, AS HIS ORCHESTRA MEMBERS rose from their seats and slowly ambled out to Coast Recorder's waiting room for their lunch break. "Asian American jazz," he went on, "has to reflect the aspirations and values of the people who create it. When we play a Duke Ellington piece, and we get to a place where he uses the blues, we might turn it into a modal section. We bring folk melodies from Asia into the jazz context, along with traditional instruments and conventions on how to improvise. Instead of a saxophone, we might use a Chinese reed trumpet or a bamboo flute."

Anthony's own background prepared the way for this musical encounter. His parents met during the postwar occupation of Japan, where his father, the son of an African American sharecropper also descended from South Carolina Choctaws, served as an Army officer. Anthony's mother came from Tokyo, and she was a passionate "jitterbugger" who haunted the American military's service clubs to catch the sounds of big band music.

"One night," said Anthony, recalling the tale that within his family has assumed the status of creation myth, "my mother and her girlfriends slipped behind the enlisted men's club. They were dancing by themselves under an open window, laughing, and causing all this commotion. My father went outside to investigate. He invited them inside. I'm the result of that episode. I truly am a child of jazz."

Anthony nodded towards the studio's folding chairs, where his wife, Martha, whose ethnic background is German and British, sat with the couple's fifteen-year-old daughter, Georgia Aiko Brown. Today marked Georgia's first recording session, though she had previously accompanied her father on percussion in local jazz clubs and music festivals.

"My father advised me not to emphasize my Japanese background," said Anthony, "because I was already going to catch hell in America for being black. But today, my daughter is the American intercultural poster child. She still has trouble at school figuring what boxes to check when they ask her to

Facing page: *Playing Brown's Rhapsodies on the Chinese violin*

145

identify her ethnicity." Anthony rolled his shoulders into a shrug and grinned. By his calculation, Georgia's background, even more complicated than his own, just compounds the cultural benefits. "She's so musically in tune," he said with fatherly pride. "At the age of five, she could tell the difference between Debussy and Ravel—between Duke Ellington and Count Basie. How many adults can do that? In so many ways, from her musicianship to the fact that she crosses all these cultural boundaries, she's a great source of my inspiration."

THE RECORDING OF *AMERICAN RHAPSODIES*—GERSHWIN'S ORIGINAL TITLE FOR *RHAPSODY IN BLUE*, WHICH Anthony has reclaimed for his ambitious revision—had proven demanding and slow-going. It was late Sunday afternoon, the middle of the long Martin Luther King Jr. holiday weekend, and the most challenging sections still required rehearsal before recording.

Back inside the studio, following lunch, the musicians all took their seats and signaled their eagerness to play, squawking, bleating, and blaring on their instruments in a round of warm-ups. The orchestra members variously speak English, Spanish, German, Chinese, Japanese, Farsi, and Tagalog, but almost no conversation took place in any language. To complete the recording, the orchestra had to work diligently through four more sections of *American Rhapsodies*—beginning with the scherzando in which Will Bernard's electric guitar improvisation takes on the central role conventionally occupied by the piano's great gale of slashing, orchestrated arpeggios.

Anthony sat down behind his trap set, raised one drumstick in his right hand, and delivered the count...

"And one, and two, and three, and four..."

Will dropped his eyes to the floor and curled into the seat of his metal folding chair as he flicked off a flurry of blues licks, the tone of his guitar laden with electrified fuzz. He riffed for several bars through the main piano theme with the muted brass wah-wahing behind him, enlivening Anthony's *American Rhapsodies* with the blues—the irreducible African American contribution to world culture merely alluded to in Gershwin's original.

"Cross-culturalization has been going on for many years," asserted Anthony, as Will set down his guitar after a perfect take. "Several of us," he recalled, "have even theorized a connection between the blues and Chinese music." In fact, much that Will had just played on electric guitar might have been rendered with equal feeling on the *erhu*, or Chinese violin—the notes momentarily bent out and back into tune, the eerie plaintive cry that recalls the human voice. "African Americans and Chinese both worked on the railroads," said Anthony, "and maybe they borrowed or just accepted each other's music because of the commonalities. Anyway," he said, gesturing with an open hand at the entire orchestra, "what all this is about is convergence."

With the sound levels set, the orchestra moved into the "love theme"—the section of *Rhapsody* now ubiquitously sampled by United Airlines advertisements—and then on through to the finale. But instead of the schmaltzy saxophone vibrato of the standard arrangement, the theme was performed with genuine mournfulness by the twining of Trinidad steel pans with the *yangqins* and a two-stringed Chinese violin. The lone violin cried out the melody, its sound pleading, raw, and unspeakably lovely. These were voicings, surely, never heard before: all the more bewitching for their clarity and their combination, each instrument rising distinctively from the ensemble even as their individual utterances coalesced into an unprecedented mix. Then the electric guitar returned, suspended midway between San Francisco and Asia: the thrumming, grinning style of the Hawai'ian slack guitar ringing out in bluesy sympathy above the tropical downpour of pinging Caribbean pans. Anthony, at last, drummed his way through these layers of sound, gongs and chugging traps suggesting the steely rhythms, the rattlety-bang of the locomotive that first inspired Gershwin eighty years ago. But this time, as the piece drove towards its climax, it was not the symphonic tympani and snare drums pushing the beat, but an array of Asian percussion—Anthony's own tom-toms pounding out hollow thunder like giant *taiko*, the huge Japanese kettle drums set on their side and hammered fiercely with mallets; his teenaged daughter rapping upon a small

Chinese flower drum shaped like a vase. And when the muted trumpets blasted their way in, raucous and blaring—it sounded as though the entire history of American music was now coming together in this room, lifted higher by the winds from China and Japan. It was the sound of cultures borrowing, blending, asserting their separate identities—all at the same time—on their way to forging something incontrovertibly new and irrepressibly alive.

E VERYTHING CHANGES. THAT'S THE LESSON FOUND IN ALMOST EVERY aspect of Bay Area life today—from birth to death and the raising of children in between. Cultures may intersect and then enthusiastically combine—or alternately strive to remain separate, seeking an impossible, debilitating purity. In any circumstance, the inexorable passage of time will prove transformative.

At the foot of the Berkeley hills stands the Nyingma Institute, the Bay Area's most prominent organization dedicated to the propagation of Tibetan Buddhism. The institute's home resembles the off-center layer-cake design of a mountainside Tibetan monastery, with its eaves, trim, and four-storied walls painted in characteristic shades of piercing red and saffron. In fact, the building is a former fraternity house.

The Nyingma Institute attracts students intent on learning how to read ancient religious texts in the original Tibetan, meditate, practice yoga, and otherwise cultivate "the logic of stillness." In the rear garden, a giant eight-sided prayer wheel spins like a mute calliope, its central mechanism and twenty-three smaller cylinders revolving ceaselessly—powered by an electric motor, which an adjacent placard praises as an unusually auspicious adaptation of western technology where wind or a down-sloping stream would ordinarily be used. The prayer wheel is a device for invoking spiritual blessings through compassion derived from the recognition of the commonality between all people—indeed, the unity that underlies the existence of all beings, from *Homo sapiens* to earthworms. In the garden stands another placard with a long list of the people responsible for building and maintaining the prayer wheel. None of the names on the list are Asian.

What remains most curious about the setting is the way it demonstrates how Tibet has imprinted its image on the Bay Area—without the benefit of a substantial body of resident Tibetans.

Only ten thousand Tibetans live in America. Only one thousand have made their way to the Bay Area. Among the thirty-two hundred students at Berkeley High School, the Tibetans number seven. Yet the Bay Area contains a plethora of Tibet-related institutions, support groups, and political action committees, including the Tibetan Association of Northern California, San Francisco Tibetan Youth Congress, and the Tibetan Nuns Project—all most publicly evident at the annual Himalayan Fair in

Tibet Uprising Day, Berkeley

THE TIBETAN MANDALA, San Francisco

Tibetan Mandala, Day One

Berkeley and Tibet Day in San Francisco. Even Tibetan commerce has caught hold. Dharma Publishing, located in Berkeley, now ranks as the nation's leading publisher of Buddhist scholarship and Tibetan history. And throughout the week, adventurous diners flock to downtown Berkeley for the delicacies of Café Tibet, presided over by a former pastry chef from San Francisco's Stars Restaurant who had previously cooked for the residents of Dharamsala, India, where the Dalai Lama and more than eight thousand other Tibetan refugees make their home.

In a sense, there exist in the Bay Area more functioning aspects of Tibetan civilization than can be found in many Tibetan villages, where the Chinese have ruthlessly suppressed the indigenous culture and religion.

Everything changes—cultures foremost—almost always with unpredictable results.

Perhaps this was the message suggested by the monks gathered in San Francisco at the California Academy of Sciences, laboring patiently over three days to construct, from millions of grains of brightly colored powders, an impossibly intricate sand mandala—the Sanskrit word for circle, community, connection. On the fourth day, they destroyed the design with equal calm and intention—a symbol of life's impermanence.

In a final gesture, the monks accepted donations and then surrendered the remnants. They swept up samples of the dispersed powders and scooped them into small manila envelopes, passing a package to each of the scores of people attending the ritual. The ceremony then complete, the observers slipped the sand into their pockets, carrying with them the materials of another culture and a glimpse of another way of life. Then they walked out into the streets of San Francisco to rejoin the unconscious enterprise of our time—the collective refashioning of American society, the many lives we might lead renewed by their very contradictions, our world about to be reborn.

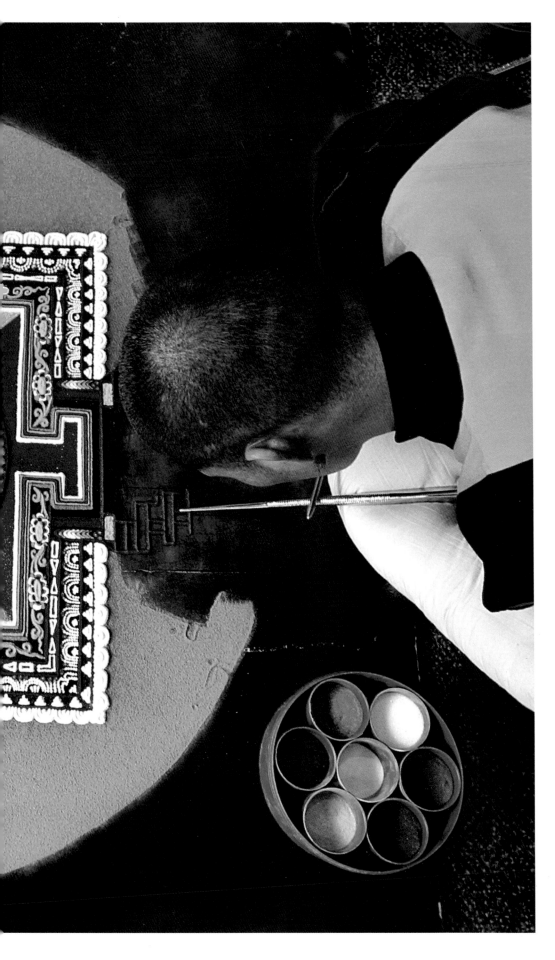

Tibetan Mandala, Day Three

Tibetan Mandala, Day Four

BOOKS

Beth Bagwell, *Oakland: The Story of a City* (Oakland, Calif.: Oakland Heritage Press, 1982)

Mark Baldassare, *California in the New Millennium* (Berkeley and Los Angeles: University of California Press, and Public Policy Institute of California, 2000)

Robert Olen Butler, *A Good Scent from a Strange Mountain* (New York: Penguin Books, 1992)

Chitra B. Divakaruni, ed., *Multitude: Cross-Cultural Readings for Writers* (New York: McGraw-Hill, 1993)

Chitra B. Divakaruni, William E. Justice, and James Quay, *California Uncovered: Stories for the 21st Century* (Berkeley: Heyday Books, 2005)

Duncan Clarke, *A New World: The History of Immigration to the United States* (San Diego: Thunder Bay Press, 2000)

Ann Douglas, *Terrible Honesty: Mongrel Manhattan in the 1920s* (New York: Farrar, Straus and Giroux, 1995)

Diana L. Eck, *A New Religious America: How a "Christian Country" Has Become the World's Most Religiously Diverse Nation* (San Francisco: HarperSan Francisco, 2001)

Anne Fadiman, *The Spirit Catches You and You Fall Down: A Hmong Child, Her American Doctors, and the Collision of Two Cultures* (New York: Farrar, Straus and Giroux, 1997)

Henry Louis Gates, Jr., *Thirteen Ways of Looking at a Black Man* (New York: Vintage Books, 1998)

Ted Gioia, *West Coast Jazz: Modern Jazz in California, 1945–1960* (Berkeley: University of California Press, 1998)

Todd Gitlin, *The Twilight of Common Dreams: Why America Is Wracked by Culture Wars* (New York: Henry Holt and Company, Inc., 1995)

Nathan Glazer, *We Are All Multiculturalists Now* (Cambridge, Mass.: Harvard University Press, 1997)

Nathan Glazer and Daniel Patrick Moynihan, *Beyond the Melting Pot: The Negroes, Puerto Ricans, Jews, Italians, and Irish of New York City* (Cambridge, Mass.: MIT Press, 1963)

José Angel Gutiérrez *A Chicano Manual on How to Handle Gringos* (Houston: Arte Publico Press, 2003)

Phillip Hammond and David Machacek, *Soka Gakkai in America: Accommodation and Conversion* (New York: Oxford University Press, 1999)

Victor Davis Hanson, *Mexifornia: A State of Becoming* (San Francisco: Encounter Books, 2003)

Woody Hochswender, Greg Martin, and Ted Morino, *The Buddha in Your Mirror: Practical Buddhism and the Search for Self* (Santa Monica, Calif.: Middleway Press, 2001)

David A. Hollinger, *PostEthnic America: Beyond Multiculturalism* (New York: Basic Books, 1995)

Marilynn S. Johnson, *The Second Gold Rush: Oakland and the East Bay in World War II* (Berkeley: University of California Press, 1993)

Tamar Jacoby, ed., *Reinventing the Melting Pot: The New Immigrants and What It Means to Be American* (New York: Basic Books, 2004)

Andrew Lam, *Perfume Dreams: Reflections on the Vietnamese Diaspora* (Berkeley: Heyday Books, 2005)

Warren Lehrer and Judith Sloan, *Crossing the BLVD: Strangers, Neighbors, Aliens in a New America* (New York: W. W. Norton, 2004)

Lawrence W. Levine, *The Opening of the American Mind: Canons, Culture, and History* (Boston: Beacon Press, 1996)

Michael Lind, *The Next American Nation: The New Nationalism and the Fourth American Revolution* (New York: Free Press, 1995)

Dale Maharidge, *The Coming White Minority: California, Multiculturalism, and America's Future* (New York: Vintage Books, 1999)

Malcolm Margolin, *The Ohlone Way: Indian Life in the San Francisco–Monterey Bay Area* (Berkeley: Heyday Books, 1978)

Rachel F. Moran, *Interracial Intimacy: The Regulation of Race and Romance* (Chicago: University of Chicago Press, 2001)

Guillermo Gomez-Peña *The New World Border: Prophecies, Poems and Loqueras for the End of the Century* (San Francisco: City Lights, 1996)

Alejandro Portes and Alex Stepick, *City on the Edge: The Transformation of Miami* (Berkeley: University of California Press, 1993)

Mary Pipher, *The Middle of Everywhere: The World's Refugees Come to Our Town* (New York: Harcourt Books, 2002)

Vijay Prashad, *Everybody Was Kung Fu Fighting: Afro-Asian Connections and the Myth of Cultural Purity* (Boston: Beacon, 2001)

Ishmael Reed, *Blues City: A Walk in Oakland* (New York: Crown Publishers, 2003)

David Rieff, *Los Angeles: Capital of the Third World* (New York: Touchstone, 1991)

Richard Rodriguez, *Days of Obligation: An Argument with My Mexican Father* (New York: Viking Press, 1992)

———, *Brown: The Last Discovery of America* (New York: Penguin Books, 2002)

Roger Sanjek, *The Future of Us All: Race and Neighborhood Politics in New York City* (Ithaca: Cornell University Press, 1998)

Orville Schell, *Virtual Tibet: Searching for Shangri-La from the Himalayas to Hollywood* (New York: Metropolitan Books, 2000)

David Schiff, *Gershwin: Rhapsody in Blue* (Cambridge: Cambridge University Press, 1997)

Peter Schrag, *Paradise Lost: California's Experience, America's Future* (Berkeley: University of California Press, 1999)

———, *California: America's High-Stakes Experiment* (Berkeley: University of California Press, 2006)

Robert O. Self, *American Babylon: Race and the Struggle for Postwar Oakland* (Princeton, N.J.: Princeton University Press, 2003)

Neil J. Smelser, William Julius Wilson, Faith Mitchell, eds., *America Becoming: Racial Trends and Their Consequences* (Washington: National Academy Press, 2001)

Roberto Suro, *Strangers Among Us: How Latino Immigration Is Transforming America* (New York: Knopf, 1998)

Kevin Starr, *Americans and the California Dream 1850–1915* (New York: Oxford University Press, 1973)

———, *Inventing the Dream: California through the Progressive Era*, (Oxford University Press, New York, 1985)

———, *Endangered Dreams: The Great Depression in California* (Oxford University Press, New York, 1996)

———, *The Dream Endures: California Enters the 1940s* (New York: Oxford University Press, 1997)

———, *Coast of Dreams: California on the Edge*, 1990–2003 (New York: Alfred A. Knopf, 2004)

Ronald Takaki, *Strangers from a Different Shore: A History of Asian Americans* (New York: Penguin Books, 1989)

Walt Whitman, *Leaves of Grass* (New York: The New American Library, 1964)

Charles Wollenberg, *Golden Gate Metropolis: Perspectives on Bay Area History* (Berkeley: University of California Institute of Governmental Studies, 1985)

REPORTS AND PAPERS

The following are available from: Public Policy Institute of California, 500 Washington Street, Suite 800, San Francisco, CA, 94111, www.ppic.org

Bruce Cain, Jack Citrin, and Cara Wong, "Ethnic Context, Race Relations, and California Politics," July 2000

Jennifer Y. Cheng, "At Home and in School: Racial and Ethnic Gaps in Educational Preparedness," November 2001

Jeffrey Grogger and Stephen J. Trejo, "Falling Behind or Moving Up? The Intergenerational Progress of Mexican Americans," May 2002

Zoltan Hajnal and Mark Baldassare, "Finding Common Ground: Racial and Ethnic Attitudes in California," March 2001

Laura E. Hill, "The Socioeconomic Well-Being of California's Immigrant Youth," July 2004

——— and Joseph M. Hayes, "California's Newest Immigrants," November 2003

———, Hans P. Johnson, and Sonya M. Tafoya, "California's Multiracial Population," August 2004

Hans Johnson, "The Demography of California Immigrants," March 2001

S. Karthick Ramakrishnan and Mark Baldassare, "The Ties That Bind: Changing Demographics and Civic Engagement in California," April 2004

Deborah Reed, "Recent Trends in Income and Poverty," February 2004

———, "The Growing Importance of Education in California," July 2003

———, "California's Rising Income Inequality: Causes and Concerns," February 1999

——— and Jennifer Cheng, "Racial and Ethnic Wage Gaps in the California Labor Market," May 2003

———, Melissa Glenn Haber, and Laura Mameesh, "The Distribution of Income in California," July 1996

——— and Richard Van Swearingen, "Poverty in California: Levels, Trends, and Demographic Dimensions," November 2001

Juan Onésimo Sandoval, Hans P. Johnson, and Sonya M. Tafoya, "Who's Your Neighbor? Residential Segregation and Diversity in California," August 2002

Sonya M. Tafoya, "The Linguistic Landscape of California Schools, "February 2002

———, "Check One or More…Mixed Race and Ethnicity in California, January 2000"

ONLINE RESOURCES

New York Times, "How Race is Lived in America," http://nytimes.com/library/national/race/

New America Media (excellent reporting on all aspects of the nation's ethnic communities, with special emphasis on California), http://news.newamericamedia.org/news/

North Gate News Online (another excellent source of news about the San Francisco Bay Area, by students at the UC Berkeley Graduate School of Journalism), http://journalism.berkeley.edu/ngno/

ABOUT THE AUTHORS

LONNY SHAVELSON IS A WRITER, PHOTOJOURNALIST, RADIO JOURNALIST, AND emergency room physician who has written and photographed stories on topics including health care in war zones, mental illness, child labor, evangelism, drug rehabilitation, assisted suicide, and health effects of hazardous waste. His articles have appeared in numerous publications, from the *New York Times* to *Mother Jones.* Shavelson's radio stories have aired on NPR, BBC/PRI *The World,* and other shows nationally. He is the author of six books, most recently *Hooked: Five Addicts Challenge Our Misguided Drug Rehab System.* Shavelson lives in Berkeley with a blind cat who loves his photographs, and way too much photography and radio production gear.

FRED SETTERBERG IS THE COAUTHOR, WITH LONNY SHAVELSON, OF *TOXIC NATION: The Fight to Save Our Communities from Chemical Contamination,* and five other books, including the award-winning *The Roads Taken: Travels through America's Literary Landscapes.* He has been a staff writer for the *East Bay Express* and editor of *Travelers' Tales America,* and has written for the *New York Times, The Nation,* and scores of other national and regional magazines.